The Basic Skills Agency

fresh start in the workplace

Getting the basics right in

Hairdressing

Mapping the Adult Literacy and Numeracy Standards to the occupational standards of the Hairdressing and Beauty Industry Authority

FOR THE USE OF TEACHING STAFF ONLY

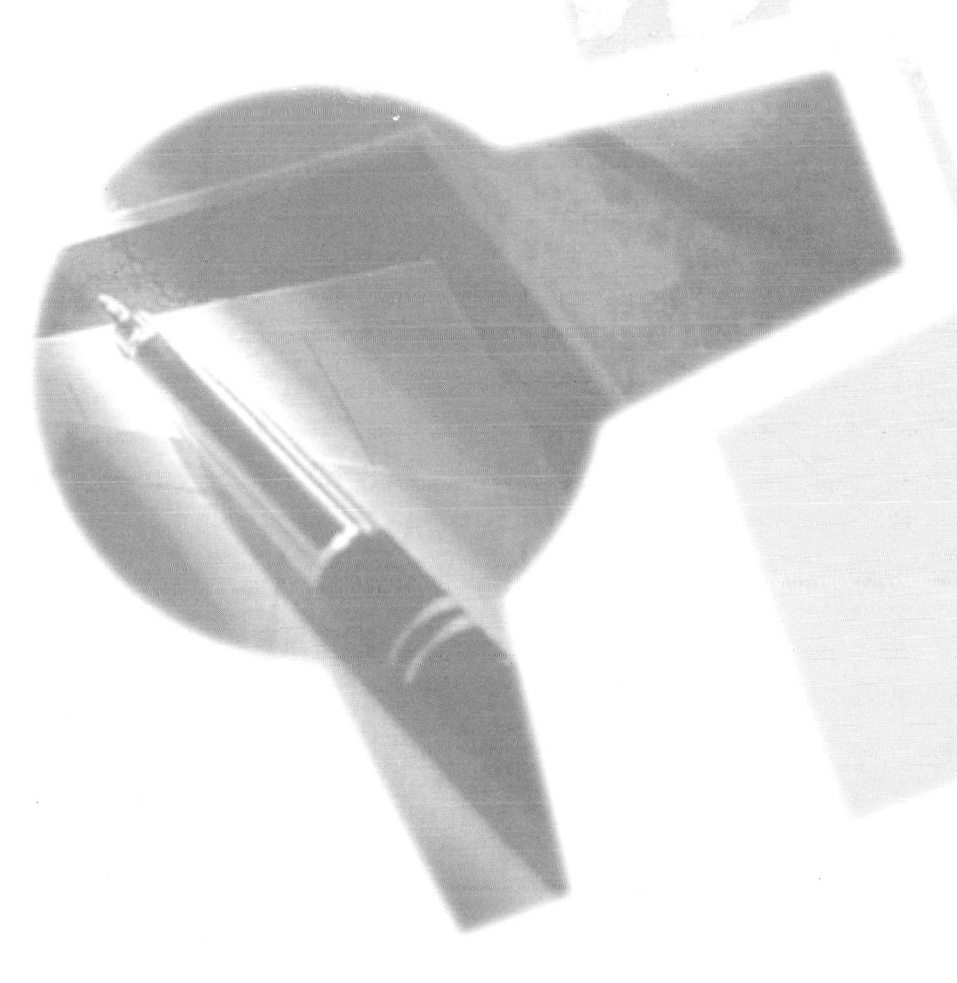

HABIA
Hairdressing And Beauty Industry Authority

Published July 2001

ISBN 1 85990 154 9

Design: Studio 21

Contents

1. Introduction

By basic skills we mean:

> *the ability to read, write and speak in English and to use mathematics at a level necessary to function and progress at work and in society in general.*

The Government's National Strategy for basic skills has identified clear targets for improving levels of literacy and numeracy amongst the general population. Research has shown that almost one in four adults has difficulties with literacy and even greater numbers need help with numeracy.

> *People at work need good basic skills not just because of the needs of a particular job. Such abilities are essential to perform a wide range of activities safely and effectively within the workplace.*
>
> *Improving literacy and numeracy – A fresh start* (DfEE, 1999)

Many of the adults with poor literacy and numeracy skills are in the workplace or are undergoing occupational training. The national strategy for improving adult literacy and numeracy skills makes clear the important contribution that can be made by National Training Organisations.

> *NTOs have a key role, and literacy and numeracy skills should be a key feature of their workforce development plans.*
>
> *Skills for Life* (DfEE, 2001)

The Basic Skills Agency has been working closely with NTOs to map their occupational standards to the *National Standards for Adult Literacy and Adult Numeracy*. These maps are intended for use in training and development for all staff within the sector.

We have worked closely with each National Training Organisation to ensure that the basic skills standards in these maps reflect the range of skills and knowledge required by workers to perform the occupational tasks.

The occupational standards, have been mapped to the *National Standards for Adult Literacy and Adult Numeracy* at the appropriate level; either Entry 3, Level 1 or Level 2. Careful account has been taken of the basic skills demands of jobs and the National Training Organisation has contributed to this process by providing examples of work instructions, health and safety guidelines and other materials in use in the workplace and in training. The National Training Organisation has also been fully involved in the process of review and evaluation of these maps at each stage.

The identification and selection of Units to be included in this document has been carried out by the NTO. The Core or Mandatory Units and Optional Units for the NVQs derived from these occupational standards are indicated on the back cover of this document. In some cases, all the necessary Units for the NVQ will be included, in others the NTO will have prioritised the most popular Units for inclusion.

National Curriculum	Literacy/Numeracy	Key Skills	National qualifications framework
		Key Skills Level 5	National qualifications framework Level 5
		Key Skills Level 4	National qualifications framework Level 4
		Key Skills Level 3	National qualifications framework Level 3
	Literacy/Numeracy Level 2	Key Skills Level 2	National qualifications framework Level 2
National Curriculum Level 5 / National Curriculum Level 4	Literacy/Numeracy Level 1	Key Skills Level 1	National qualifications framework Level 1
National Curriculum Level 3	Literacy/Numeracy Entry 3		Entry Level
National Curriculum Level 2	Literacy/Numeracy Entry 2		
National Curriculum Level 1	Literacy/Numeracy Entry 1		

2. Workplace basic skills

How many employees have difficulties with basic skills?

23% of people of working age have low levels of literacy and numeracy – almost 7 million people.

> **Fact**
>
> All countries have problems with poor literacy and numeracy, but the UK, when compared with other developed nations, has more problems than most – 23% with very low literacy skills in the UK, compared with 7% in Sweden and 12% in Germany.
>
> *Source: Adult Literacy in Britain, ONS*

What does this mean in real numbers of employees?

Population of England	49.3 million
61.4% of working age (16-59/64)	30.27 million
23% of people of working age are likely to have 'very poor' basic skills	6.96 million

Source: Adult Literacy in Britain, ONS

It is a fact that in small and medium sized businesses, over 2 million workers are likely to have poor basic skills. In large organisations a further 2 million employees have difficulties with basic skills and in the public sector there are a million more workers with poor basic skills.

What are the consequences of poor basic skills amongst employees?

Workers with poor basic skills are at a considerable disadvantage in the workplace. Research has shown that employees with basic skills difficulties:

- will be less likely to receive work-related training;
- will have a limited number of jobs open to them;
- may find themselves vulnerable in times of change;
- often turn down promotion because they are afraid of the paperwork;
- will often be in lower paid jobs.

What are the consequences for employers?

Many of the problems experienced at work are linked to poor basic skills. Training, health and safety, quality procedures and many more issues are affected by employees who lack the skills to deal with the requirements of the workplace. Poor basic skills may mean:

- poor productivity;
- administration errors with customer orders;
- increased wastage rates;
- poor customer relations;

- incorrect production of orders;
- increased machine downtime;
- inefficiency of production or provision of services;
- increased staff turnover;
- difficulties over the introduction of new methods of working and new technology;
- external recruitment instead of internal promotion.

And what about the economy?

The Moser Report, *Improving literacy and numeracy – A fresh start,* published in 1999, suggested that poor basic skills might be one of the reasons for low productivity in the UK economy.

> '‘At work, basic skills matter crucially. They are a key to employability ... And there is evidence that they are growing in importance, employers rate them ever more highly. Moreover, poor basic skills affect the efficiency and competitiveness of the economy. The pace of development and change in business is undermined. They represent a significant cost to British industry. ’

> A report, quoted by David Blunkett in 1997, suggested that poor literacy costs business and government £10 billion every year.
>
> Source: *Education and Training and their Impact on the Economy,* Ernst and Young

What are the benefits of providing training and improving the levels of basic skills amongst workers?

- Ability to improve performance and meet targets
- Increased efficiency and productivity
- Improved staff retention and commitment
- Improved staff take-up and benefit from training
- Ability to re-deploy staff
- Improved customer service
- Improved skills and confidence amongst workers
- Increased ability to perform jobs to national standards and achieve accreditation

3. Mapping rationale

How many Adult Literacy and Numeracy Standards are shown for each occupational standard of work?

The mapping has been carried out using a number of factors in order to decide the appropriate choice of Adult Literacy and Numeracy Standards. In collaboration with the NTO, we have decided on the **main**, or **critical**, basic skills required in order to perform each of the performance criteria or work standards.

In some cases, there will be only one Adult Literacy and Numeracy Standard mapped, for example, *Reading* in order to follow straightforward work instructions. For other performance criteria, more than one Adult Literacy and Numeracy Standard will be included in the map, for example, *Speaking and listening* and *Writing* will be shown when a worker has to make a report both verbally and in writing.

Which Adult Literacy and Numeracy Standard statements have been used and why?

As a general rule, in these maps the main purpose of the work standard has been the guiding factor in deciding which of the following basic skills statements is used.

Speaking and Listening

- *Speak to communicate* – if the main purpose of the task is to give information.
- *Listen and respond* – if the main purpose is to receive or gain information.
- *Engage in discussion* – in cases where there is a requirement to engage in an exchange of information.

Reading

- *Read and understand* – in instances when the worker needs to read a range of texts in order to gain understanding about concepts or principles.
- *Read and obtain information* – when the worker needs to follow a set of guidelines or written instructions in order to complete a task or procedure.

Writing

- *Write to communicate* – this statement covers all the occasions when a worker would need to write in order to perform a task. The appropriate descriptor would then apply eg information, ideas or opinions, depending on the context.

Numeracy

- *Understanding and using mathematical information* – this statement has generally been used to describe tasks where information, problems or instructions are given in numerical form (a product specification, product codes, charts and timetables).
- *Calculating and manipulating mathematical information* – is used when actual calculations have to be done and results are generated (calibrating a machine, weighing items, handling money).
- *Interpreting results and communicating mathematical information* – this is used when a task involves reporting or recording mathematical information (stock control sheets, quality data sheets).

Which level has been chosen and why?

Three levels from the Standards have been used in these maps.

- *Entry 3* – this level includes work tasks involving text, writing and numeracy in familiar and everyday contexts and of limited length.

- *Level 1* – this level has been chosen to describe the skills required to perform routine and straightforward work tasks of varying length.

- *Level 2* – this is used where tasks at work are more complex or non-routine.

4. Guidelines for use

How to use the grids

The basic skills grids provide an 'at-a-glance' overview of the range and levels of basic skills required for each unit. From this section you can move to the detailed information about basic skills in the maps, for the purposes of training or staff development. The diagram below illustrates how to use the grids.

Basic Skills Grid

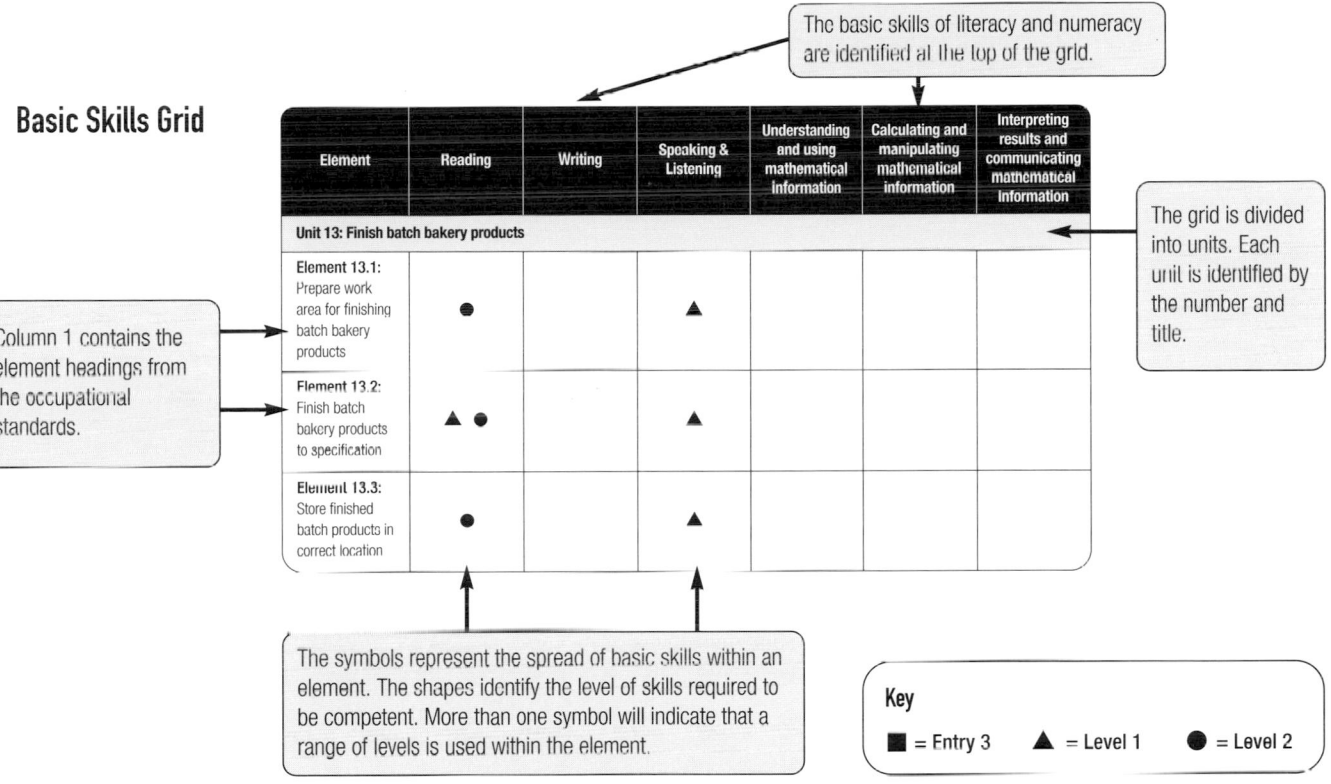

The basic skills of literacy and numeracy are identified at the top of the grid.

The grid is divided into units. Each unit is identified by the number and title.

Column 1 contains the element headings from the occupational standards.

The symbols represent the spread of basic skills within an element. The shapes identify the level of skills required to be competent. More than one symbol will indicate that a range of levels is used within the element.

Key
■ = Entry 3   ▲ = Level 1   ● = Level 2

How to use the maps

The maps are presented at Element level with all the national standards of work mapped to the required Adult Literacy and Numeracy Standards at the appropriate level. The diagram below illustrates how to use the map to identify the skills and levels of reading, writing, speaking and listening and number that underpin the occupational standards.

Basic Skills Map

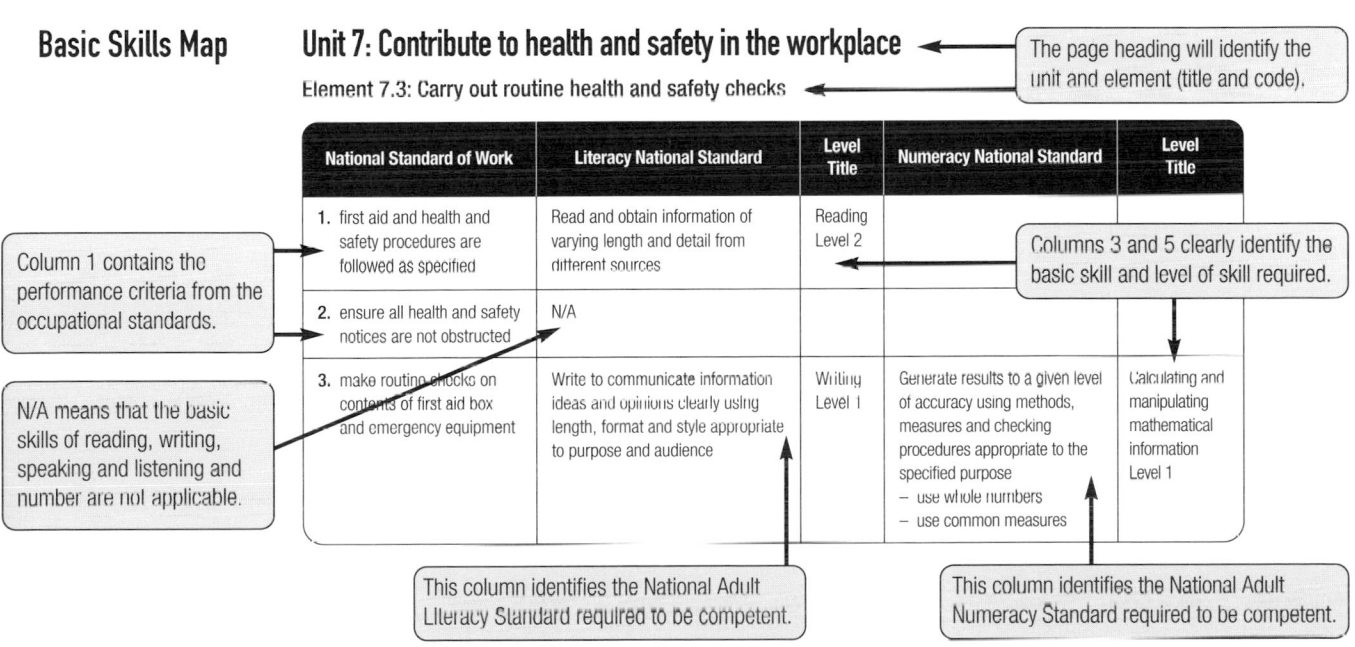

The page heading will identify the unit and element (title and code).

Columns 3 and 5 clearly identify the basic skill and level of skill required.

Column 1 contains the performance criteria from the occupational standards.

N/A means that the basic skills of reading, writing, speaking and listening and number are not applicable.

This column identifies the National Adult Literacy Standard required to be competent.

This column identifies the National Adult Numeracy Standard required to be competent.

Progression from the Adult Literacy and Numeracy Standards to the Adult Literacy and Numeracy Core Curriculum

In Sections 7 and 8 of this document you will find:

• an overview of the Adult Literacy and Numeracy Standards used in the maps;

• progression tables in speaking and listening, reading and writing, number, measures, shape and space and handling data.

The progression tables include:

• all the curriculum elements demonstrating the skills and knowledge required for teaching and learning;

• the curriculum references that lead you directly to the required part of the Adult Literacy and Numeracy Core Curriculum documents.

This diagram illustrates how the progression works.

Element 9.1: Process valid passenger tickets and passes

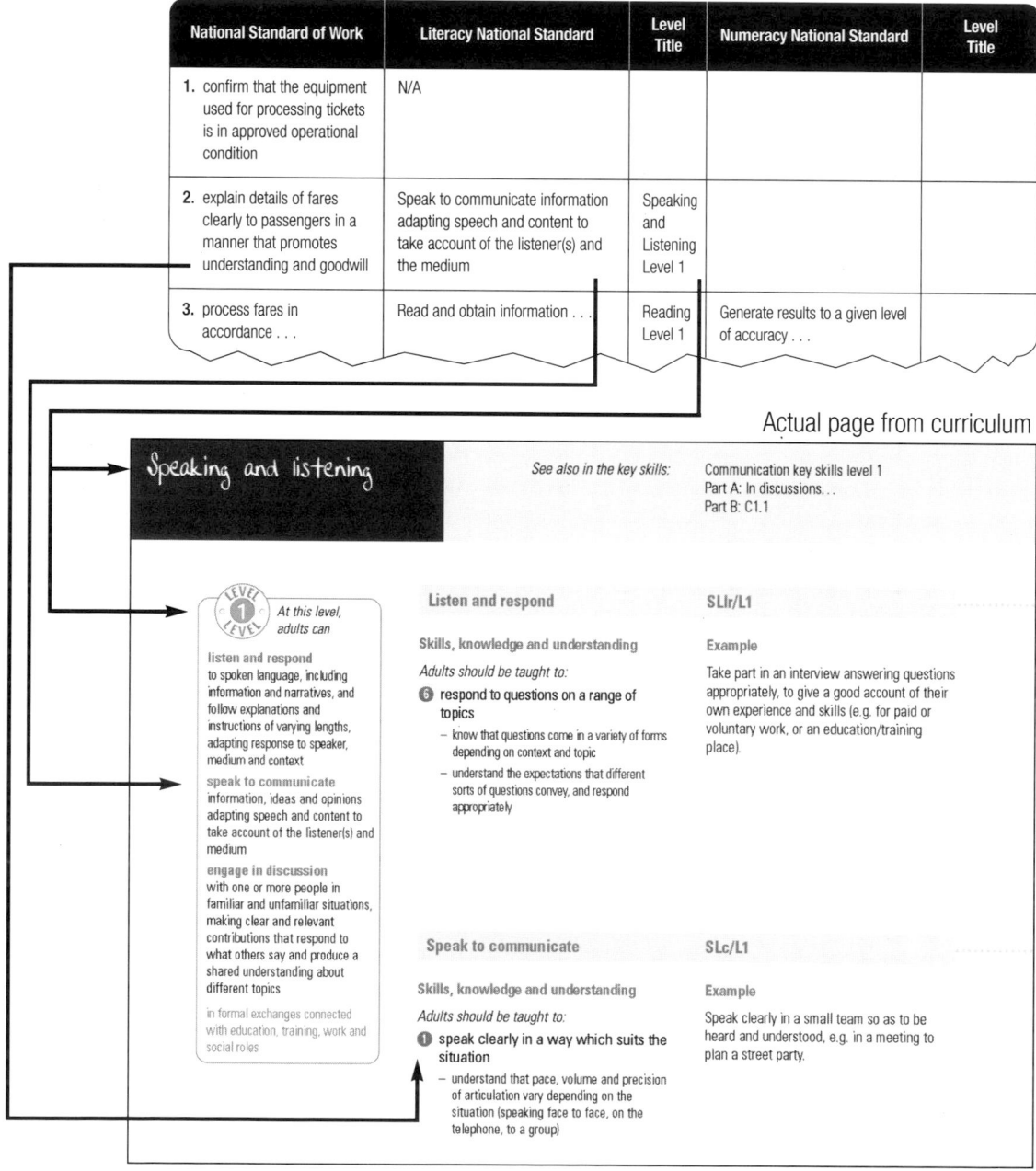

National Standard of Work	Literacy National Standard	Level Title	Numeracy National Standard	Level Title
1. confirm that the equipment used for processing tickets is in approved operational condition	N/A			
2. explain details of fares clearly to passengers in a manner that promotes understanding and goodwill	Speak to communicate information adapting speech and content to take account of the listener(s) and the medium	Speaking and Listening Level 1		
3. process fares in accordance . . .	Read and obtain information . . .	Reading Level 1	Generate results to a given level of accuracy . . .	

Actual page from curriculum

Speaking and listening

See also in the key skills: Communication key skills level 1
Part A: In discussions...
Part B: C1.1

LEVEL 1 At this level, adults can

listen and respond to spoken language, including information and narratives, and follow explanations and instructions of varying lengths, adapting response to speaker, medium and context

speak to communicate information, ideas and opinions adapting speech and content to take account of the listener(s) and medium

engage in discussion with one or more people in familiar and unfamiliar situations, making clear and relevant contributions that respond to what others say and produce a shared understanding about different topics

in formal exchanges connected with education, training, work and social roles

Listen and respond　　　SLlr/L1

Skills, knowledge and understanding

Adults should be taught to:

⑥ respond to questions on a range of topics
– know that questions come in a variety of forms depending on context and topic
– understand the expectations that different sorts of questions convey, and respond appropriately

Example

Take part in an interview answering questions appropriately, to give a good account of their own experience and skills (e.g. for paid or voluntary work, or an education/training place).

Speak to communicate　　　SLc/L1

Skills, knowledge and understanding

Adults should be taught to:

❶ speak clearly in a way which suits the situation
– understand that pace, volume and precision of articulation vary depending on the situation (speaking face to face, on the telephone, to a group)

Example

Speak clearly in a small team so as to be heard and understood, e.g. in a meeting to plan a street party.

5. Basic Skills Grids

an overview of each Unit

Element	Reading	Writing	Speaking & Listening	Understanding and using mathematical information	Calculating and manipulating mathematical information	Interpreting results and communicating mathematical information
Unit 201: Advise and consult with clients						
Element 201.1: Consult with and maintain effective working relationships with clients	●	▲	▲		▲	
Element 201.2: Advise clients on salon products and services	●	▲	▲ ●			
Element 201.3: Advise clients on after-care procedures	●		▲ ●			
Unit 202: Shampoo and condition hair and scalp						
Element 202.1: Maintain effective and safe methods of working when shampooing and conditioning hair	●	▲	▲		■ ▲	■
Element 202.2: Shampoo hair and scalp	▲		■			
Element 202.3: Condition hair and scalp	▲ ●		▲			

Element	Reading	Writing	Speaking & Listening	Understanding and using mathematical information	Calculating and manipulating mathematical information	Interpreting results and communicating mathematical information
Unit 203: Style hair using drying and setting techniques						
Element 203.1: Maintain effective and safe methods of working when styling hair	●	▲	▲	●	▲	■
Element 203.2: Dry and finish hair to style	▲ ●		▲	▲		
Element 203.3: Set and dress hair to style	●		▲	▲	■	
Element 203.4: Dress long hair to style	●		▲			
Unit 204: Cut hair using basic techniques						
Element 204.1: Maintain effective and safe methods of working when cutting hair	●				▲	
Element 204.2: Cut hair to achieve a variety of one length looks	●		▲		■	
Element 204.3: Cut hair to achieve a variety of layered looks	●		▲		■	

Element	Reading	Writing	Speaking & Listening	Understanding and using mathematical information	Calculating and manipulating mathematical information	Interpreting results and communicating mathematical information
Unit 205A: Perm and neutralise hair						
Element 205A.1: Maintain effective and safe methods of working when perming and neutralising hair	▲ ●	▲	▲	▲	■ ▲	■
Element 205A.2: Perm hair using basic techniques	●		▲		▲	
Element 205A.3: Neutralise hair	●		■ ▲	▲	▲	
Unit 205B: Perm, relax and neutralise hair						
Element 205B.1: Maintain effective and safe methods of working when perming, relaxing and neutralising hair	▲ ●	▲	▲	▲	■ ▲	■
Element 205B.2: Perm hair using basic techniques	●		▲	▲	▲	
Element 205B.3: Relax hair	●		▲		▲	
Element 205B.4: Neutralise hair	▲ ●		■ ▲		▲	

Element	Reading	Writing	Speaking & Listening	Understanding and using mathematical information	Calculating and manipulating mathematical information	Interpreting results and communicating mathematical information
Unit 206: Change hair colour using basic techniques						
Element 206.1: Maintain effective and safe methods of working when colouring hair	▲ ●	▲	▲	▲	■ ▲ ●	■ ▲
Element 206.2: Add colour to hair	●	▲	▲		▲	▲
Element 206.3: Permanently change hair colour	●	▲	▲		▲ ●	▲
Element 206.4: Create highlight and lowlight effects in hair	●	▲	▲		▲ ●	▲
Unit 207: Fulfil salon reception duties						
Element 207.1: Attend to clients and enquiries		■ ▲	▲		■	
Element 207.2: Make appointments for salon services		■	▲		▲	■
Element 207.3: Handle payments from clients for the purchase of services and retail products	▲	▲	▲		▲	

Element	Reading	Writing	Speaking & Listening	Understanding and using mathematical information	Calculating and manipulating mathematical information	Interpreting results and communicating mathematical information
Unit 208: Develop and maintain effective team work and relationships						
Element 208.1: Develop and maintain effective team work and relationships with colleagues	●		▲ ●			
Element 208.2: Develop and improve personal effectiveness within the job role	●	●	▲ ●			
Unit 209: Support health, safety and security of the salon environment						
Element 209.1: Follow emergency procedures	▲ ●	●	▲ ●			
Element 209.2: Support health, safety and security at work	▲ ●	▲	▲			
Unit 210: Cut hair using barbering techniques						
Element 210.1: Maintain effective and safe methods of working when cutting hair using barbering techniques	●				▲	
Element 210.2: Cut hair to achieve a variety of looks with different neckline shapes	●		▲			

Element	Reading	Writing	Speaking & Listening	Understanding and using mathematical information	Calculating and manipulating mathematical information	Interpreting results and communicating mathematical information
Unit 211: Provide shaving and face massage services						
Element 211.1: Maintain effective and safe methods of working when shaving and massaging the face	▲ ●	▲	▲ ●		■ ▲	
Element 211.2: Remove hair by shaving	▲ ●		▲			
Element 211.3: Massage the face	▲		▲			
Unit 212: Cut facial hair to shape						
Element 212.1: Maintain effective and safe methods of working when cutting facial hair	●		▲		▲	
Element 212.2: Cut beards and moustaches to shape	●		▲			
Unit 213: Dry hair into shape and create a finished look						
Element 213.1: Maintain effective and safe methods of working when drying hair	●	▲	▲		■ ▲	
Element 213.2: Dry and finish hair	▲ ●		▲			

6. Basic Skills Maps

detailed maps of the Performance Criteria in each Element

Unit 201: Advise and consult with clients

Element 201.1: Consult with and maintain effective working relationships with clients

National Standard of Work	Literacy National Standard	Level Title	Numeracy National Standard	Level Title
a. the client's wishes for services and products are clearly identified	Engage in discussion with one or more people in familiar and unfamiliar situations, making clear and relevant contributions that respond to what others say and produce a shared understanding about different topics.	Speaking and Listening Level 1		
b. the client is encouraged to ask about areas of which they are unsure	Engage in discussion with one or more people in familiar and unfamiliar situations, making clear and relevant contributions that respond to what others say and produce a shared understanding about different topics.	Speaking and Listening Level 1		
c. factors that limit or affect services and choice of products are accurately identified	Read and obtain information of varying length and detail from different sources.	Reading Level 2		
d. any necessary tests or visual checks on hair, skin and scalp are conducted in accordance with specified procedures	Read and understand a range of texts of varying complexity accurately and independently.	Reading Level 2	Generate results to a given level of accuracy using given methods, measures and checking procedures appropriate to the specified purpose – use common measures.	Calculating and manipulating mathematical information Level 1
e. any problems identified which cannot be dealt with are reported promptly to the relevant person	Speak to communicate information, ideas and opinions adapting speech and content to take account of the listener(s) and medium.	Speaking and Listening Level 1		
f. the agreed services, products and the likely outcome are acceptable to the client and meet their needs	Engage in discussion with one or more people in familiar and unfamiliar situations, making clear and relevant contributions that respond to what others say and produce a shared understanding about different topics.	Speaking and Listening Level 1		

National Standard of Work	Literacy National Standard	Level Title	Numeracy National Standard	Level Title
g. the cost and likely duration of agreed services is clearly stated and confirmed with the client	Engage in discussion with one or more people in familiar and unfamiliar situations, making clear and relevant contributions that respond to what others say and produce a shared understanding about different topics.	Speaking and Listening Level 1	Generate results to a given level of accuracy using given methods, measures and checking procedures appropriate to the specified purpose – use common measures.	Calculating and manipulating mathematical information Level 1
h. all communication with the client is conducted effectively and in a manner that maintains client goodwill, trust and confidentiality	Engage in discussion with one or more people in familiar and unfamiliar situations, making clear and relevant contributions that respond to what others say and produce a shared understanding about different topics.	Speaking and Listening Level 1		
i. client records are up to date, accurate, easy to read and complete	Write to communicate information, ideas and opinions clearly using length, format and style appropriate to purpose and audience.	Writing Level 1		

Unit 201: Advise and consult with clients

Element 201.2: Advise clients on salon products and services

National Standard of Work	Literacy National Standard	Level Title	Numeracy National Standard	Level Title
a. opportunities for the promotion of services and products are identified and followed up	Read and understand a range of texts of varying complexity accurately and independently. Engage in discussion with one or more people in familiar and unfamiliar situations, making clear and relevant contributions that respond to what others say and produce a shared understanding about different topics.	Reading Level 2 Speaking and Listening Level 1		
b. the features and benefits of the products and services are clearly and accurately stated	Speak to communicate information, ideas and opinions adapting speech and content to take account of the listener(s) and medium.	Speaking and Listening Level 1		
c. advice and information provided to clients encourages return visits	Speak to communicate information, ideas and opinions adapting speech and content to take account of the listener(s) and medium.	Speaking and Listening Level 1		
d. all communication with clients is conducted effectively and in a manner that maintains client goodwill and trust	Engage in discussion with one or more people in a variety of different situations, making clear and effective contributions that produce outcomes appropriate to purpose and topic.	Speaking and Listening Level 2		
e. records are up to date, accurate, easy to read and complete	Write to communicate information, ideas and opinions clearly using length, format and style appropriate to purpose and audience.	Writing Level 1		

Unit 201: Advise and consult with clients

Element 201.3: Advise clients on after-care procedures

National Standard of Work	Literacy National Standard	Level Title	Numeracy National Standard	Level Title
a. advice and recommendations are relevant to the individual client	Engage in discussion with one or more people in familiar and unfamiliar situations, making clear and relevant contributions that respond to what others say and produce a shared understanding about different topics.	Speaking and Listening Level 1		
b. after-care advice and recommendations are accurate, constructive and based on an up to date knowledge of the technical services and products available	Read and obtain information of varying length and detail from different sources.

Engage in discussion with one or more people in a variety of different situations, making clear and effective contributions that produce outcomes appropriate to purpose and topic. | Reading Level 2

Speaking and Listening Level 2 | | |
c. the client is encouraged to ask about areas of which they are unsure	Engage in discussion with one or more people in familiar and unfamiliar situations, making clear and relevant contributions that respond to what others say and produce a shared understanding about different topics.	Speaking and Listening Level 1		
d. clients are actively encouraged to follow the recommended after-care procedures	Speak to communicate information, ideas and opinions adapting speech and content to take account of the listener(s) and medium.	Speaking and Listening Level 1		
e. all communication with clients is conducted effectively and in a manner that maintains client goodwill, trust and confidentiality	Engage in discussion with one or more people in familiar and unfamiliar situations, making clear and relevant contributions that respond to what others say and produce a shared understanding about different topics.	Speaking and Listening Level 1		

Unit 202: Shampoo and condition hair and scalp

Element 202.1: Maintain effective and safe methods of working when shampooing and conditioning hair

National Standard of Work	Literacy National Standard	Level Title	Numeracy National Standard	Level Title
a. the preparation of the client meets salon requirements	N/A			
b. products and equipment used are based on the result of consultation with the client	Engage in discussion with one or more people in familiar and unfamiliar situations, making clear and relevant contributions that respond to what others say and produce a shared understanding about different topics.	Speaking and Listening Level 1		
c. equipment, when used, is suitable for achieving the desired result	N/A			
d. your work methods ensure the health and safety of the client and yourself	Read and obtain information of varying length and detail from different sources.	Reading Level 2		
e. your work methods minimise wastage of products	N/A			
f. organisation of your work activities ensures effective use of all working time			Generate results to a given level of accuracy using given methods, measures and checking procedures appropriate to the specified purpose – use common measures.	Calculating and manipulating mathematical information Level 1
g. your work area is kept clean, tidy and free of waste	N/A			
h. your standards of health and hygiene minimise risk of cross infection and infestation	Read and obtain information of varying length and detail from different sources.	Reading Level 2		
i. low levels of products and towels are replenished as required			Generate results to a given level of accuracy using given methods, measures and checking procedures appropriate to the specified purpose – use whole numbers.	Calculating and manipulating mathematical information Entry 3

Getting the basics right in Hairdressing

National Standard of Work	Literacy National Standard	Level Title	Numeracy National Standard	Level Title
j. products needing re-ordering are identified and reported to the relevant person	Speak to communicate information, ideas and opinions adapting speech and content to take account of the listener(s) and medium.	Speaking and Listening Level 1	Present and explain results that meet the intended purpose using appropriate numbers, diagrams, charts and symbols.	Calculating and manipulating mathematical information Entry 3
k. client records, where required, are accurate, complete, easy to read and up to date	Write to communicate information, ideas and opinions clearly using length, format and style appropriate to purpose and audience.	Writing Level 1		

Unit 202: Shampoo and condition hair and scalp

Element 202.2: Shampoo hair and scalp

National Standard of Work	Literacy National Standard	Level Title	Numeracy National Standard	Level Title
a. preparation activities meet salon and service requirements	Read and understand straightforward texts of varying length on a variety of topics accurately and independently.	Reading Level 1		
b. scalp massage techniques are adapted to meet the needs of the hair and scalp condition and hair length	Read and obtain information from different sources.	Reading Level 1		
c. the water temperature and flow suit the needs of the hair and scalp and the comfort of the client	Speak to communicate information, feelings and opinions on familiar topics, using appropriate formality, both face to face and on the telephone.	Speaking and Listening Entry 3		
d. hair and scalp are left clean and free from shampoo	N/A			
e. the hair is left free of excess moisture	N/A			
f. the hair is combed through without causing damage to the hair or scalp	N/A			

Getting the basics right in Hairdressing

Unit 202: Shampoo and condition hair and scalp

Element 202.3: Condition hair and scalp

National Standard of Work	Literacy National Standard	Level Title	Numeracy National Standard	Level Title
a. preparation activities meet salon and service requirements	Read and understand straightforward texts of varying length on a variety of topics accurately and independently.	Reading Level 1		
b. conditioning products used are based on the result of the consultation with the client	Engage in discussion with one or more people in familiar and unfamiliar situations, making clear and relevant contributions that respond to what others say and produce a shared understanding about different topics.	Speaking and Listening Level 1		
c. the application, massage and removal of conditioning treatment meets the needs of the hair and scalp and manufacturers' instructions	Read and understand a range of texts of varying complexity accurately and independently.	Reading Level 2		
d. the hair is left free of excess moisture	N/A			
e. the hair is combed through without causing damage to the hair or scalp	N/A			

Unit 203: Style hair using drying and setting techniques

Element 203.1: Maintain effective and safe methods of working when styling hair

National Standard of Work	Literacy National Standard	Level Title	Numeracy National Standard	Level Title
a. the preparation of the client meets salon requirements	N/A			
b. the products, tools and equipment used are suitable for achieving the desired look	Read and obtain information of varying length and detail from different sources.	Reading Level 2	Specify and describe a practical activity, problem or task using mathematical information and language to increase understanding and select appropriate methods for carrying through a substantial activity.	Understanding and using mathematical information Level 2
c. your work methods ensure the health and safety of the client and yourself	Read and obtain information of varying length and detail from different sources.	Reading Level 2		
d. the organisation of your work activities ensures effective use of all working time			Generate results to a given level of accuracy using methods, measures and checking procedures appropriate to the specified purpose – use common measures.	Calculating and manipulating mathematical information Level 1
e. the work area is kept clean, tidy and free of waste	N/A			
f. your work methods minimise the risk of damage to tools	N/A			
g. your standards of health and hygiene minimise the risk of cross infection and infestation	Read and obtain information of varying length and detail from different sources.	Reading Level 2		
h. low level of products are identified and reported to the relevant person	Speak to communicate information, ideas and opinions adapting speech and content to take account of the listener(s) and medium. Write to communicate information, ideas and opinions clearly using length, format and style appropriate to purpose and audience.	Speaking and Listening Level 1 Writing Level 1	Present and explain results that meet the intended purpose using appropriate numbers, diagrams, charts and symbols.	Interpreting results and communicating mathematical information Entry 3

Getting the basics right in Hairdressing

Unit 203: Style hair using drying and setting techniques

Element 203.2: Dry and finish hair to style

National Standard of Work	Literacy National Standard	Level Title	Numeracy National Standard	Level Title
a. preparation activities meet salon, service and legal requirements	Read and obtain information of varying length and detail from different sources.	Reading Level 2		
b. the client's wishes for the desired look are clearly identified before drying	Engage in discussion with one or more people in familiar and unfamiliar situations, making clear and relevant contributions that respond to what others say and produce a shared understanding about different topics.	Speaking and Listening Level 1		
c. drying and finishing techniques used are suitable for achieving the desired look	Read and obtain information from different sources.	Reading Level 1		
d. the application of products, when used, meets manufacturers' instructions	Read and understand range of texts of varying complexity accurately and independently	Reading Level 2	Specify and describe a practical activity, problem or task using mathematical information and language to make accurate observations and identify suitable calculations to achieve an appropriate outcome.	Understanding and using mathematical information Level 1
e. the hair is effectively controlled, dried and finished taking account of critical influencing factors	Read and obtain information of varying length and detail from different sources.	Reading Level 2		
f. the client's requirements are confirmed during the drying process	Engage in discussion with one or more people in familiar and unfamiliar situations, making clear and relevant contributions that respond to what others say and produce a shared understanding about different topics.	Speaking and Listening Level 1		
g. the client's position is adjusted and drying techniques are adapted as necessary to assist styling	N/A			

Unit 203: Style hair using drying and setting techniques

Element 203.2: Dry and finish hair to style *(continued)*

National Standard of Work	Literacy National Standard	Level Title	Numeracy National Standard	Level Title
h. the finished look is to the satisfaction of the client	Speak to communicate information, ideas and opinions adapting speech and content to take account of the listener(s) and medium.	Speaking and Listening Level 1		

Getting the basics right in Hairdressing

Unit 203: Style hair using drying and setting techniques

Element 203.3: Set and dress hair to style

National Standard of Work	Literacy National Standard	Level Title	Numeracy National Standard	Level Title
a. preparation activities meet salon, service and legal requirements	Read and obtain information of varying length and detail from different sources.	Reading Level 2		
b. the client's wishes are clearly identified before setting	Engage in discussion with one or more people in familiar and unfamiliar situations, making clear and relevant contributions that respond to what others say and produce a shared understanding about different topics.	Speaking and Listening Level 1		
c. the hair is effectively controlled and set taking into account critical influencing factors	Read and obtain information of varying length and detail from different sources.	Reading Level 2		
d. the application of products, when used, meets manufacturers' instructions	Read and understand a range of texts of varying complexity accurately and independently.	Reading Level 2	Specify and describe a practical activity, problem or task using mathematical information and language to make accurate observations and identify suitable calculations to achieve an appropriate outcome.	Understanding and using mathematical information Level 1
e. setting techniques used are suitable for achieving the desired look	Read and obtain information of varying length and detail from different sources.	Reading Level 2	Generate results to a given level of accuracy using given methods, measures and checking procedures appropriate to the specified purpose – use space and shape.	Calculating and manipulating mathematical information Entry 3
f. setting techniques avoid damage to the hair, skin and scalp	N/A			
g. the hair is dried, when required, prior to dressing out	N/A			
h. items used for setting are removed avoiding discomfort to the client	N/A			

Unit 203: Style hair using drying and setting techniques

Element 203.3: Set and dress hair to style *(continued)*

National Standard of Work	Literacy National Standard	Level Title	Numeracy National Standard	Level Title
i. the dressing techniques used achieve the desired look	N/A			
j. the finished look is to the satisfaction of the client	Engage in discussion with one or more people in familiar and unfamiliar situations, making clear and relevant contributions that respond to what others say and produce a shared understanding about different topics.	Speaking and Listening Level 1		

Unit 203: Style hair using drying and setting techniques

Element 203.4: Dress long hair to style

National Standard of Work	Literacy National Standard	Level Title	Numeracy National Standard	Level Title
a. the hair is prepared to meet style requirements	N/A			
b. the client's wishes for the desired look are clearly identified before dressing	Engage in discussion with one or more people in familiar and unfamiliar situations, making clear and relevant contributions that respond to what others say and produce a shared understanding about different topics.	Speaking and Listening Level 1		
c. the hair is effectively controlled and secured into place	N/A			
d. equipment used to secure the hair is not visible unless part of the style requirements	N/A			
e. finishing products are used and applied effectively to meet manufacturers' instructions	Read and obtain information of varying length and detail from different sources.	Reading Level 2		
f. the finished style takes into account critical influencing factors	Read and obtain information of varying length and detail from different sources.	Reading Level 2		
g. the finished style is to the satisfaction of the client	Engage in discussion with one or more people in familiar and unfamiliar situations, making clear and relevant contributions that respond to what others say and produce a shared understanding about different topics.	Speaking and Listening Level 1		

Unit 204: Cut hair using basic techniques

Element 204.1: Maintain effective and safe methods of working when cutting hair

National Standard of Work	Literacy National Standard	Level Title	Numeracy National Standard	Level Title
a. the preparation of the client meets salon requirements	N/A			
b. the tools used are suitable for achieving the desired look	N/A			
c. your work methods ensure the health and safety of the client and yourself	Read and obtain information of varying length and detail from different sources.	Reading Level 2		
d. the organisation of your work activities ensures effective use of all working time			Generate results to a given level of accuracy using methods, measures and checking procedures appropriate to the specified purpose – use common measures.	Calculating and manipulating mathematical information Level 1
e. your work area is kept clean, tidy and free of waste	N/A			
f. your working methods minimise the risk of damage to tools	N/A			
g. your standards of health and hygiene minimise risk of cross infection and infestation	Read and obtain information of varying length and detail from different sources.	Reading Level 2		
h. used sharps are disposed of to meet legal and salon requirements	Read and obtain information of varying length and detail from different sources.	Reading Level 2		

Unit 204: Cut hair using basic techniques

Element 204.2: Cut hair to achieve a variety of one length looks

National Standard of Work	Literacy National Standard	Level Title	Numeracy National Standard	Level Title
a. preparation activities meet salon, service and legal requirements	Read and obtain information of varying length and detail from different sources.	Reading Level 2		
b. the desired look is confirmed with the client prior to cutting	Engage in discussion with one or more people in familiar and unfamiliar situations, making clear and relevant contributions that respond to what others say and produce a shared understanding about different topics.	Speaking and Listening Level 1		
c. cutting techniques are suitable for the client's hair and to achieve the desired look			Generate results to a given level of accuracy using methods, measures and checking procedures appropriate to the specified purpose – use space and shape.	Calculating and manipulating mathematical information Entry 3
d. cutting techniques are adapted to take into account critical influencing factors	Read and obtain information of varying length and detail from different sources.	Reading Level 2	Generate results to a given level of accuracy using methods, measures and checking procedures appropriate to the specified purpose – use common measures – use space and shape.	Calculating and manipulating mathematical information Entry 3
e. hair cuttings which may affect the comfort of the client are promptly removed	N/A			
f. the client is consulted during the cutting process to confirm the desired look	Engage in discussion with one or more people in familiar and unfamiliar situations, making clear and relevant contributions that respond to what others say and produce a shared understanding about different topics.	Speaking and Listening Level 1		
g. the finished one length look is accurately cut and is to the satisfaction of the client	Engage in discussion with one or more people in familiar and unfamiliar situations, making clear and relevant contributions that respond to what others say and produce a shared understanding about different topics.	Speaking and Listening Level 1		

Unit 204: Cut hair using basic techniques

Element 204.3: Cut hair to achieve a variety of layered looks

National Standard of Work	Literacy National Standard	Level Title	Numeracy National Standard	Level Title
a. preparation activities meet salon service and legal requirements	Read and obtain information of varying length and detail from different sources.	Reading Level 2		
b. the desired look is confirmed with the client prior to cutting	Engage in discussion with one or more people in familiar and unfamiliar situations, making clear and relevant contributions that respond to what others say and produce a shared understanding about different topics.	Speaking and Listening Level 1		
c. cutting techniques are adapted to take into account critical influencing factors, hair type and the cutting effect required	Read and obtain information of varying length and detail from different sources.	Reading Level 2	Generate results to a given level of accuracy using methods, measures and checking procedures appropriate to the specified purpose – use space and shape.	Calculating and manipulating mathematical information Entry 3
d. hair cuttings which may affect the comfort of the client are promptly removed	N/A			
e. the client is consulted during the cutting process to confirm the desired look	Engage in discussion with one or more people in familiar and unfamiliar situations, making clear and relevant contributions that respond to what others say and produce a shared understanding about different topics.	Speaking and Listening Level 1		
f. the finished layered look is cut accurately and is to the satisfaction of the client	Engage in discussion with one or more people in familiar and unfamiliar situations, making clear and relevant contributions that respond to what others say and produce a shared understanding about different topics.	Speaking and Listening Level 1		

Unit 205A: Perm and neutralise hair

Element 205A.1: Maintain effective and safe methods of working when perming and neutralising hair

National Standard of Work	Literacy National Standard	Level Title	Numeracy National Standard	Level Title
a. the preparation of the client meets salon requirements	N/A			
b. your choice of products, tools and equipment used are based on the results of any necessary tests and consultation with client	Read and obtain information of varying length and detail from different sources. Engage in familiar discussion with one or more people in familiar and unfamiliar situations, making clear and relevant contributions that respond to what others say and produce a shared understanding about different topics.	Reading Level 2 Speaking and Listening Level 1	Specify and describe a practical activity, problem or task using mathematical information and language to make accurate observations and identify suitable calculations to achieve an appropriate outcome.	Understanding and using mathematical information Level 1
c. product preparation meets manufacturer's instructions	Read and understand a range of texts of varying complexity accurately and independently.	Reading Level 2	Generate results to a given level of accuracy using methods, measures and checking procedures appropriate to the specified purpose – use common measures.	Calculating and manipulating mathematical information Level 1
d. any necessary tests on hair are conducted in accordance with specified procedures	Read and understand a range of texts of varying complexity accurately and independently.	Reading Level 2	Generate results to a given level of accuracy using methods, measures and checking procedures appropriate to the specified purpose use common measures.	Calculating and manipulating mathematical information Level 1
e. your work methods ensure the health and safety of the client and yourself	Read and obtain information of varying length and detail from different sources.	Reading Level 2		
f. personal protective equipment is used to meet legal and salon requirements	Read and obtain information from different sources.	Reading Level 1		
g. organisation of your work activities ensures effective use of all working time			Generate results to a given level of accuracy using methods, measures and checking procedures appropriate to the specified purpose – use common measures.	Calculating and manipulating mathematical information Level 1

Unit 205A: Perm and neutralise hair

Element 205A.1: Maintain effective and safe methods of working when perming and neutralising hair *(continued)*

National Standard of Work	Literacy National Standard	Level Title	Numeracy National Standard	Level Title
h. the work area is kept clean, tidy and free of waste	N/A			
i. low levels of sundries are replenished as required			Generate results to a given level of accuracy using given methods, measures and checking procedures appropriate to the specified purpose – use whole numbers – use common measures.	Calculating and manipulating mathematical information Entry 3
j. products which need to be re-ordered are identified and reported to the relevant person	Speak to communicate information, ideas and opinions adapting speech and content to take account of the listener(s) and medium. Write to communicate information, ideas and opinions clearly using length, format and style appropriate to purpose and audience.	Speaking and Listening Level 1 Writing Level 1	Present and explain results that meet the intended purpose using appropriate numbers, diagrams, charts and symbols.	Interpreting results and communicating mathematical information Entry 3
k. your working methods minimise wastage and the risk of damage to tools and equipment	N/A			
l. products are used and disposed of to meet manufacturers' and legal requirements	Read and obtain information of varying length and detail from different sources.	Reading Level 2		
m. client records are accurate, easy to read and up to date	Write to communicate information, ideas and opinions clearly using length, format and style appropriate to purpose and audience.	Writing Level 1	Present and explain results that meet the intended purpose using appropriate numbers, diagrams, charts and symbols.	Interpreting results and communicating mathematical information Entry 3

Unit 205A: Perm and neutralise hair

Element 205A.2: Perm hair using basic techniques

National Standard of Work	Literacy National Standard	Level Title	Numeracy National Standard	Level Title
a. preparation activities meet salon, service and legal requirements	Read and obtain information of varying length and detail from different sources.	Reading Level 2		
b. the desired effect is confirmed with the client prior to perming	Engage in discussion with one or more people in familiar and unfamiliar situations, making clear and relevant contributions that respond to what others say and produce a shared understanding about different topics.	Speaking and Listening Level 1		
c. use of products and techniques take into account critical influencing factors	Read and obtain information of varying length and detail from different sources.	Reading Level 2		
d. the sectioning and winding techniques used achieve the desired effect	N/A			
e. the application of products meets manufacturer's instructions	Read and understand a range of texts of varying complexity accurately and independently.	Reading Level 2	Generate results to a given level of accuracy using methods, measures and checking procedures appropriate to the specified purpose – use common measures.	Calculating and manipulating mathematical information Level 1
f. the perm is monitored accurately and a development test curl taken as required			Generate results to a given level of accuracy using methods, measures and checking procedures appropriate to the specified purpose – use common measures.	Calculating and manipulating mathematical information Level 1
g. any problems identified during the perming process are resolved within limits of your own authority	Read and understand range of texts of varying complexity accurately and independently.	Reading Level 2		

Unit 205A: Perm and neutralise hair

Element 205A.2: Perm hair using basic techniques *(continued)*

National Standard of Work	Literacy National Standard	Level Title	Numeracy National Standard	Level Title
h. problems which cannot be resolved are referred promptly to the relevant person for action	Speak to communicate information, ideas and opinions adapting speech and content to take account of the listener(s) and medium.	Speaking and Listening Level 1		
i. the hair is left free of perm lotion when the desired degree of curl is accurately established	N/A			

Unit 205A: Perm and neutralise hair

Element 205A.3: Neutralise hair

National Standard of Work	Literacy National Standard	Level Title	Numeracy National Standard	Level Title
a. preparation activities meet salon, service and legal requirements	Read and obtain information of varying length and detail from different sources.	Reading Level 2		
b. the water temperature and flow suit the needs of the hair and scalp, and the comfort of the client	Speak to communicate information, feelings and opinions on familiar topics, using appropriate formality, both face to face and on the telephone.	Speaking and Listening Entry 3		
c. the hair is free from chemicals and excess moisture prior to the application of the neutralising agent	N/A			
d. the distribution of neutralising agent is even and in accordance with manufacturers' instructions	Read and understand a range of texts of varying complexity accurately and independently.	Reading Level 2	Specify and describe a practical activity, problem or task using mathematical information and language to make accurate observations and identify suitable calculations to achieve an appropriate outcome.	Understanding and using mathematical information Level 1
e. the neutralising process is timed in accordance with manufacturers' instructions			Generate results to a given level of accuracy using methods, measures and checking procedures appropriate to the specified purpose.	Calculating and manipulating mathematical information Level 1
f. the hair is left free from all traces of the neutralising agent	N/A			
g. rods are removed without disturbing the curl formation	N/A			
h. any problems identified during the neutralising process are resolved, if possible, within the limits of your own authority	Read and understand a range of texts of varying complexity accurately and independently.	Reading Level 2		
i. problems which cannot be resolved are referred promptly to the relevant person for action	Speak to communicate information, ideas and opinions adapting speech and content to take account of the listener(s) and medium.	Speaking and Listening Level 1		

Unit 205B: Perm, relax and neutralise hair

Element 205B.1: Maintain effective and safe methods of working when perming, relaxing and neutralising hair

National Standard of Work	Literacy National Standard	Level Title	Numeracy National Standard	Level Title
a. the preparation of the client meets salon requirements	N/A			
b. your choice of products, tools and equipment used are based on the results of any necessary tests and consultation with client	Read and obtain information of varying length and detail from different sources. Engage in familiar discussion with one or more people in familiar and unfamiliar situations, making clear and relevant contributions that respond to what others say and produce a shared understanding about different topics.	Reading Level 2 Speaking and Listening Level 1	Specify and describe a practical activity, problem or task using mathematical information and language to make accurate observations and identify suitable calculations to achieve an appropriate outcome.	Understanding and using mathematical information Level 1
c. product preparation meets manufacturer's instructions	Read and understand a range of texts of varying complexity accurately and independently.	Reading Level 2	Generate results to a given level of accuracy using methods, measures and checking procedures appropriate to the specified purpose.	Calculating and manipulating mathematical information Level 1
d. any necessary tests on hair are conducted in accordance with specified procedures	Read and understand a range of texts of varying complexity accurately and independently.	Reading Level 2	Generate results to a given level of accuracy using methods, measures and checking procedures appropriate to the specified purpose.	Calculating and manipulating mathematical information Level 1
e. your work methods ensure the health and safety of the client and yourself	Read and obtain information of varying length and detail from different sources.	Reading Level 2		
f. personal protective equipment is used to meet legal and salon requirements	Read and obtain information from different sources.	Reading Level 1		
g. organisation of your work activities ensures effective use of all working time			Generate results to a given level of accuracy using methods, measures and checking procedures appropriate to the specified purpose – use common measures.	Calculating and manipulating mathematical information Level 1

Getting the basics right in Hairdressing

National Standard of Work	Literacy National Standard	Level Title	Numeracy National Standard	Level Title
h. the work area is kept clean, tidy and free of waste	N/A			
i. low levels of sundries are replenished as required			Generate results to a given level of accuracy using methods, measures and checking procedures appropriate to the specified purpose – use whole numbers – use common measures.	Calculating and manipulating mathematical information Entry 3
j. products needing re-ordering are identified and reported to the relevant person	Speak to communicate information, ideas and opinions adapting speech and content to take account of the listener(s) and medium. Write to communicate information, ideas and opinions clearly using length, format and style appropriate to purpose and audience.	Speaking and Listening Level 1 Writing Level 1	Present and explain results that meet the intended purpose using appropriate numbers, diagrams, charts and symbols.	Interpreting results and communicating mathematical information Entry 3
k. your working methods minimise wastage and the risk of damage to tools and equipment	N/A			
l. products are used and disposed of to meet manufacturers' and legal requirements	Read and obtain information of varying length and detail from different sources.	Reading Level 2		
m. client records are up to date, accurate, easy to read and complete	Write to communicate information, ideas and opinions clearly using length, format and style appropriate to purpose and audience.	Writing Level 1	Present and explain results that meet the intended purpose using appropriate numbers, diagrams, charts and symbols.	Interpreting results and communicating mathematical information Entry 3

Unit 205B: Perm, relax and neutralise hair

Element 205B.2: Perm hair using basic techniques

National Standard of Work	Literacy National Standard	Level Title	Numeracy National Standard	Level Title
a. preparation activities meet salon, service and legal requirements	Read and understand range of texts of varying complexity accurately and independently.	Reading Level 2		
b. the desired effect is confirmed with the client prior to perming	Engage in discussion with one or more people in familiar and unfamiliar situations, making clear and relevant contributions that respond to what others say and produce a shared understanding about different topics.	Speaking and Listening Level 1		
c. use of products and techniques take into account critical influencing factors	Read and obtain information of varying length and detail from different sources.	Reading Level 2		
d. hair structure is rearranged, when necessary, prior to winding	N/A			
e. the sectioning and winding techniques used achieve the desired effect	N/A			
f. the application of products meets the needs of the hair and manufacturers' instructions	Read and understand a range of texts of varying complexity accurately and independently.	Reading Level 2	Read and understand straightforward mathematical information used for different purposes and independently select relevant information from given graphical, numerical and written material.	Understanding and using mathematical information Level 1
g. the perm is monitored accurately and a development test curl taken as required			Generate results to a given level of accuracy using methods, measures and checking procedures appropriate to the specified purpose.	Calculating and manipulating mathematical information Level 1
h. any problems identified during the perming process are resolved within the limits of your own authority	Read and understand a range of texts of varying complexity accurately and independently.	Reading Level 2		

Getting the basics right in Hairdressing

National Standard of Work	Literacy National Standard	Level Title	Numeracy National Standard	Level Title
i. problems which cannot be resolved are referred promptly to the relevant person for action	Speak to communicate information, ideas and opinions adapting speech and content to take account of the listener(s) and medium.	Speaking and Listening Level 1		
j. the permed hair is left free of perm lotion when the desired degree of curl is accurately established	N/A			

Unit 205B: Perm, relax and neutralise hair

Element 205B.3: Relax hair

National Standard of Work	Literacy National Standard	Level Title	Numeracy National Standard	Level Title
a. preparation activities meet salon, service and legal requirements	Read and obtain information of varying length and detail from different sources.	Reading Level 2		
b. the desired effect is confirmed with the client prior to relaxing	Engage in discussion with one or more people in familiar and unfamiliar situations, making clear and relevant contributions that respond to what others say and produce a shared understanding about different topics.	Speaking and Listening Level 1		
c. the application of relaxing products takes into account the manufacturers' instructions	Read and understand a range of texts of varying complexity accurately and independently.	Reading Level 2	Generate results to a given level of accuracy using methods, measures and checking procedures appropriate to the specified purpose.	Calculating and manipulating mathematical information Level 1
d. hair is relaxed taking into account critical influencing factors	Read and obtain information of varying length and detail from different sources.	Reading Level 2		
e. the relaxing process is monitored continually and strand test conducted as required			Generate results to a given level of accuracy using methods, measures and checking procedures appropriate to the specified purpose – use common measures.	Calculating and manipulating mathematical information Level 1
f. the relaxed hair is left free of all visible traces of relaxing agent with the required degree of reduced curl	N/A			
g. any problems identified during the relaxing process are resolved, if possible, within limits of own authority	Read and understand a range of texts of varying complexity accurately and independently.	Reading Level 2		
h. problems which cannot be resolved are referred promptly to the relevant person for action	Speak to communicate information, ideas and opinions adapting speech and content to take account of the listener(s) and medium.	Speaking and Listening Level 1		

Unit 205B: Perm, relax and neutralise hair

Element 205B.4: Neutralise hair

National Standard of Work	Literacy National Standard	Level Title	Numeracy National Standard	Level Title
a. preparation activities meet salon, service and legal requirements.	Read and obtain information of varying length and detail from different sources.	Reading Level 2		
b. the neutralising agent used is compatible with the previous system	Read and obtain information from different sources.	Reading Level 1		
c. the water temperature and flow suit the needs of the hair and scalp and the comfort of the client	Speak to communicate information, feelings and opinions on familiar topics, using appropriate formality, both face to face and on the telephone.	Speaking and Listening Entry 3		
d. the relaxer, when used, is removed without causing unnecessary scalp irritation	N/A.			
e. the hair is free from chemicals and excess moisture, where necessary, prior to the application of the neutralising agent	N/A			
f. the distribution of the neutralising agent is even and in accordance with manufacturer's instructions	Read and understand a range of texts of varying complexity accurately and independently.	Reading Level 2	Generate results to a given level of accuracy using methods, measures and checking procedures appropriate to the specified purpose – use common measures.	Calculating and manipulating mathematical information Level 1
g. the neutralising process is timed accurately and repeated, where necessary, according to manufacturer's instructions	Read and understand a range of texts of varying complexity accurately and independently.	Reading Level 2	Generate results to a given level of accuracy using methods, measures and checking procedures appropriate to the specified purpose.	Calculating and manipulating mathematical information Level 1
h. the hair is left free from all traces of the neutralising agent	N/A			
i. the rods, when used, are removed without adversely affecting the formed wave movement	N/A			

Unit 205B: Perm, relax and neutralise hair

Element 205B.4: Neutralise hair *(continued)*

National Standard of Work	Literacy National Standard	Level Title	Numeracy National Standard	Level Title
j. the selection, application and removal of conditioner, when used, meets manufacturer's instructions	Read and understand a range of texts of varying complexity accurately and independently.	Reading Level 2		
k. any problems identified during the neutralising process are resolved, if possible, within limits of own authority	Read and understand straightforward texts of varying length on a variety of topics accurately and independently.	Reading Level 1		
l. problems which cannot be resolved are referred promptly to the relevant person for action	Speak to communicate information, ideas and opinions adapting speech and content to take account of the listener(s) and medium.	Speaking and Listening Level 1		

Unit 206.1: Change hair colour using basic techniques

Element 206.1: Maintain effective and safe methods of working when colouring hair

National Standard of Work	Literacy National Standard	Level Title	Numeracy National Standard	Level Title
a. the preparation of the client meets salon requirements	N/A			
b. products, tools and equipment used are based on the results of any necessary tests and consultation with the client	Read and obtain information of varying length and detail from different sources. Engage in discussion with one or more people in familiar and unfamiliar situations, making clear and relevant contributions that respond to what others say and produce a shared understanding about different topics.	Reading Level 2 Speaking and Listening Level 1	Specify and describe a practical activity, problem or task using mathematical information and language to make accurate observations and identify suitable calculations to achieve an appropriate outcome.	Understanding and using mathematical information Level 1
c. product preparation meets with manufacturers' instructions	Read and understand a range of texts of varying complexity accurately and independently.	Reading Level 2	Generate results to an appropriate level of accuracy using methods, measures and checking procedures appropriate to the specified purpose – use common measures.	Calculating and manipulating mathematical information Level 2
d. the necessary tests on hair and skin are conducted in accordance with specified procedures	Read and understand a range of texts of varying complexity accurately and independently.	Reading Level 2	Generate results to an appropriate level of accuracy using methods, measures and checking procedures appropriate to the specified purpose – use common measures.	Calculating and manipulating mathematical information Level 1
e. your work methods ensure the health and safety of the client and yourself	Read and obtain information of varying length and detail from different sources.	Reading Level 2		
f. personal protective equipment is used to meet legal and salon requirements	Read and obtain information from different sources.	Reading Level 1		
g. the organisation of your work activities ensures effective use of all working time			Generate results to an appropriate level of accuracy using methods, measures and checking procedures appropriate to the specified purpose – use common measures.	Calculating and manipulating mathematical information Level 1

Unit 206.1: Change hair colour using basic techniques

Element 206.1: Maintain effective and safe methods of working when colouring hair *(continued)*

National Standard of Work	Literacy National Standard	Level Title	Numeracy National Standard	Level Title
h. your work area is clean, tidy and free of waste	N/A			
i. low levels of sundries are replenished as required			Generate results to a given level of accuracy using given methods, measures and checking procedures appropriate to the specified purpose – use common measures.	Calculating and manipulating mathematical information Entry 3
j. products which need to be re-ordered are identified and reported to the relevant person	Speak to communicate information, ideas and opinions adapting speech and content to take account of the listener(s) and medium. Write to communicate information, ideas and opinions clearly using length, format and style appropriate to purpose and audience.	Speaking and Listening Level 1 Writing Level 1	Present and explain results that meet the intended purpose using appropriate numbers, diagrams, charts and symbols.	Interpreting results and communicating mathematical information Entry 3
k. your working methods minimise wastage and the risk of damage to tools and equipment	N/A			
l. products are used and disposed of to meet manufacturers' and legal requirements	Read and obtain information of varying length and detail from different sources.	Reading Level 2		
m. client records are accurate, complete and up to date	Write to communicate information, ideas and opinions clearly using length, format and style appropriate to purpose and audience.	Writing Level 1	Present and explain results that meet the intended purpose using an appropriate format to a given level of accuracy.	Interpreting results and communicating mathematical information Level 1

Unit 206: Change hair colour using basic techniques

Element 206.2: Add colour to hair

National Standard of Work	Literacy National Standard	Level Title	Numeracy National Standard	Level Title
a. preparation activities meet salon, service and legal requirements	Read and obtain information of varying length and detail from different sources.	Reading Level 2		
b. the desired effect is confirmed with the client prior to the application of colour	Engage in discussion with one or more people in familiar and unfamiliar situations, making clear and relevant contributions that respond to what others say and produce a shared understanding about different topics.	Speaking and Listening Level 1		
c. your choice and application of colour is accurate and takes account of critical influencing factors	Read and obtain information of varying length and detail from different sources.	Reading Level 2		
d. the techniques used minimise the risk of colour being spread to client's skin, clothes and surrounding areas	N/A			
e. the development of colour is monitored accurately as required			Generate results to a given level of accuracy using given methods, measures and checking procedures appropriate to the specified purpose – use common measures.	Calculating and manipulating mathematical information Level 1
f. the hair and scalp are left free of colouring products, when required, after the desired effect is achieved	N/A			
g. any problems identified during the colouring process are resolved, if possible, within limits of own authority	Read and obtain information of varying length and detail from different sources	Reading Level 2		

Unit 206: Change hair colour using basic techniques

Element 206.2: Add colour to hair *(continued)*

National Standard of Work	Literacy National Standard	Level Title	Numeracy National Standard	Level Title
h. problems which cannot be resolved are referred promptly to the relevant person for action	Speak to communicate information, ideas and opinions adapting speech and content to take account of the listener(s) and medium.	Speaking and Listening Level 1		
i. the finished colouring effect is to the satisfaction of the client	Engage in discussion with one or more people in familiar and unfamiliar situations, making clear and relevant contributions that respond to what others say and produce a shared understanding about different topics.	Speaking and Listening Level 1		
j. client records are up to date, accurate, easy to read and complete	Write to communicate information ideas and opinions clearly using length, format and style appropriate to purpose and audience.	Writing Level 1	Present and explain results that meet the intended purpose using an appropriate format to a given level of accuracy.	Interpreting results and communicating mathematical information Level 1

Unit 206: Change hair colour using basic techniques

Element 206.3: Permanently change hair colour

National Standard of Work	Literacy National Standard	Level Title	Numeracy National Standard	Level Title
a. preparation activities meet salon, service and legal requirements	Read and obtain information of varying length and detail from different sources.	Reading Level 2		
b. the desired effect is confirmed with the client prior to application of colour	Engage in discussion with one or more people in familiar and unfamiliar situations, making clear and relevant contributions that respond to what others say and produce a shared understanding about different topics.	Speaking and Listening Level 1		
c. your choice and application of colour is accurate and takes account of critical influencing factors	Read and obtain information of varying length and detail from different sources.	Reading Level 2		
d. product use meets with manufacturers' instructions	Read and understand a range of texts of varying complexity accurately and independently.	Reading Level 2	Generate results to a given level of accuracy using methods, measures and checking procedures appropriate to the specified purpose – use common measures.	Calculating and manipulating mathematical information Level 2
e. the hair is sectioned accurately in order to achieve the desired effect required	N/A			
f. techniques used minimise the risk of the product being spread to client's skin, clothes and surrounding areas	N/A			
g. the development of the product is monitored accurately as required			Generate results to a given level of accuracy using methods, measures and checking procedures appropriate to the specified purpose – use common measures.	Calculating and manipulating mathematical information Level 1

Unit 206: Change hair colour using basic techniques

Element 206.3: Permanently change hair colour *(continued)*

National Standard of Work	Literacy National Standard	Level Title	Numeracy National Standard	Level Title
h. the hair and scalp are left free of colouring products as soon as the desired effect has been achieved	N/A			
i. any problems identified during the colouring process are resolved, if possible, within limits of own authority	Read and obtain information of varying length and detail from different sources.	Reading Level 2		
j. problems which cannot be resolved are referred promptly to the relevant person for action	Speak to communicate information, ideas and opinions adapting speech and content to take account of the listener(s) and medium.	Speaking and Listening Level 1		
k. the finished effect is to the satisfaction of the client	Speak to communicate information, ideas and opinions adapting speech and content to take account of the listener(s) and medium.	Speaking and Listening Level 1		
l. client records are up to date, accurate, easy to read and complete	Write to communicate information, ideas and opinions clearly using length, format and style appropriate to purpose and audience.	Writing Level 1	Present and explain results that meet the intended purpose using appropriate numbers, diagrams, charts and symbols.	Interpreting results and communicating mathematical information Entry 3

Unit 206: Change hair colour using basic techniques

Element 206.4: Create highlight and lowlight effects in hair

National Standard of Work	Literacy National Standard	Level Title	Numeracy National Standard	Level Title
a. preparation activities meet salon, service and legal requirements	Read and obtain information of varying length and detail from different sources.	Reading Level 2		
b. the desired effect and technique to be used is confirmed with the client prior to the application of colour	Engage in discussion with one or more people in familiar and unfamiliar situations, making clear and relevant contributions that respond to what others say and produce a shared understanding about different topics.	Speaking and Listening Level 1		
c. the technique used is suitable to create the desired effect	N/A			
d. your choice and application of colour is accurate and takes account of the critical influencing factors	Read and obtain information of varying length and detail from different sources.	Reading Level 2		
e. product use meets manufacturers' instructions	Read and understand a range of texts of varying complexity accurately and independently.	Reading Level 2	Generate results to a given level of accuracy using methods, measures and checking procedures appropriate to the specified purpose – use common measures.	Calculating and manipulating mathematical information Level 2
f. the hair to be processed is accurately selected to enable the desired effect to be achieved	N/A			
g. the techniques used minimise the risk of product being spread to client's skin, clothes and surrounding areas	N/A			
h. the development of the product is monitored accurately			Generate results to a given level of accuracy using methods, measures and checking procedures appropriate to the specified purpose.	Calculating and manipulating mathematical information Level 1

Unit 206: Change hair colour using basic techniques

Element 206.4: Create highlight and lowlight effects in hair *(continued)*

National Standard of Work	Literacy National Standard	Level Title	Numeracy National Standard	Level Title
i. the product removal, where necessary, avoids disturbance to further development	N/A			
j. any problems identified during the process are resolved, if possible, within limits of own authority	Read and understand a range of texts of varying complexity accurately and independently.	Reading Level 2		
k. problems which cannot be resolved are referred promptly to the relevant person for action	Speak to communicate information, ideas and opinions adapting speech and content to take account of the listener(s) and medium.	Speaking and Listening Level 1		
l. the finished effect is to the satisfaction of the client	Engage in discussion with one or more people in familiar and unfamiliar situations, making clear and relevant contributions that respond to what others say and produce a shared understanding about different topics.	Speaking and Listening Level 1		
m. client records are up to date, accurate, easy to read and complete	Write to communicate information, ideas and opinions clearly using length, format and style appropriate to purpose and audience.	Writing Level 1	Present and explain results that meet the intended purpose using appropriate numbers, diagrams, charts and symbols.	Interpreting results and communicating mathematical information Entry 3

Unit 207: Fulfil salon reception duties

Element 207.1: Attend to clients and enquiries

National Standard of Work	Literacy National Standard	Level Title	Numeracy National Standard	Level Title
a. all people making enquiries are treated in a polite manner	Engage in discussion with one or more people in familiar and unfamiliar situations, making clear and relevant contributions that respond to what others say and produce a shared understanding about different topics.	Speaking and Listening Level 1		
b. the purpose of the enquiry is correctly identified	Speak to communicate information, ideas and opinions adapting speech and content to take account of the listener(s) and medium.	Speaking and Listening Level 1		
c. appointments are confirmed and the relevant staff member is promptly informed	Write to communicate information and opinions with some adaptation to the intended audience. Speak to communicate information, ideas and opinions adapting speech and content to take account of the listener(s) and medium.	Writing Entry 3 Speaking and Listening Level 1		
d. enquiries which cannot be dealt with are referred promptly to the relevant person for action	Speak to communicate information, ideas and opinions adapting speech and content to take account of the listener(s) and medium.	Speaking and Listening Level 1		
e. messages taken are recorded accurately and passed to the relevant person at the right time	Write to communicate information, ideas and opinions clearly using length, format and style appropriate to purpose and audience. Speak to communicate information, ideas and opinions adapting speech and content to take account of the listener(s) and medium.	Writing Level 1 Speaking and Listening Level 1		
f. information given is clear and accurate	Write to communicate information, ideas and opinions clearly using length, format and style appropriate to purpose and audience.	Writing Level 1	Generate results to a given level of accuracy using given methods, measures and checking procedures appropriate to the specified purpose.	Calculating and manipulating mathematical information Entry 3

Unit 207: Fulfil salon reception duties

Element 207.1: Attend to clients and enquiries *(continued)*

National Standard of Work	Literacy National Standard	Level Title	Numeracy National Standard	Level Title
g. confidential information is only given to authorised people	Speak to communicate information, ideas and opinions adapting speech and content to take account of the listener(s) and medium.	Speaking and Listening Level 1		

Unit 207: Fulfil salon reception duties

Element 207.2: Make appointments for salon services

National Standard of Work	Literacy National Standard	Level Title	Numeracy National Standard	Level Title
a. all requests for appointments are dealt with politely and promptly	Engage in discussion with one or more people in familiar and unfamiliar situations, making clear and relevant contributions that respond to what others say and produce a shared understanding about different topics.	Speaking and Listening Level 1		
b. client requirements relating to the service requested are accurately identified	Engage in discussion with one or more people in familiar and unfamiliar situations, making clear and relevant contributions that respond to what others say and produce a shared understanding about different topics.	Speaking and Listening Level 1		
c. appointments are scheduled to satisfy the client and to ensure the most productive use of salon time			Generate results to a given level of accuracy using methods, measures and checking procedures appropriate to the specified purpose – use common measures.	Calculating and manipulating mathematical information Level 1
d. the availability of services is confirmed, where necessary, with relevant colleagues	Engage in discussion with one or more people in familiar and unfamiliar situations, making clear and relevant contributions that respond to what others say and produce a shared understanding about different topics.	Speaking and Listening Level 1		
e. appointment details are confirmed as acceptable to the client	Engage in discussion with one or more people in familiar and unfamiliar situations, making clear and relevant contributions that respond to what others say and produce a shared understanding about different topics.	Speaking and Listening Level 1		
f. all appointment details are accurate, recorded in the right place and are easy to read	Write to communicate information and opinions with some adaptation to the intended audience.	Writing Entry 3	Present and explain results that meet the intended purpose using appropriate numbers, diagrams, charts and symbols.	Interpreting results and communicating mathematical information Entry 3

Unit 207: Fulfil salon reception duties

Element 207.3: Handle payments from clients for the purchase of services and retail products

National Standard of Work	Literacy National Standard	Level Title	Numeracy National Standard	Level Title
a. costs to the client are totalled accurately			Generate results to a given level of accuracy using methods, measures and checking procedures appropriate to the specified purpose – use common measures.	Calculating and manipulating mathematical information Level 1
b. the client is informed of the cost in a courteous manner	Engage in discussion with one or more people in familiar and unfamiliar situations, making clear and relevant contributions that respond to what others say and produce a shared understanding about different topics.	Speaking and Listening Level 1		
c. the client's method of payment is established and receipt of payment is acknowledged	Speak to communicate information, ideas and opinions adapting speech and content to take account of the listener(s) and medium.	Speaking and Listening Level 1		
d. payments are checked as correct			Generate results to a given level of accuracy using methods, measures and checking procedures appropriate to the specified purpose – use common measures.	Calculating and manipulating mathematical information Level 1
e. relevant documents are accurately completed	Write to communicate information, ideas and opinions clearly using length, format and style appropriate to purpose and audience.	Writing Level 1		
f. any discrepancies in payments are identified and resolved, if possible, within limits of your own authority	Speak to communicate information, ideas and opinions adapting speech and content to take account of the listener(s) and medium.	Speaking and Listening Level 1	Generate results to a given level of accuracy using methods, measures and checking procedures appropriate to the specified purpose – use common measures.	Calculating and manipulating mathematical information Level 1
g. payment discrepancies which cannot be resolved are referred promptly to the relevant person for action	Speak to communicate information, ideas and opinions adapting speech and content to take account of the listener(s) and medium.	Speaking and Listening Level 1		

Getting the basics right in Hairdressing

National Standard of Work	Literacy National Standard	Level Title	Numeracy National Standard	Level Title
h. correct change is given and receipts issued as required	Write to communicate information, ideas and opinions clearly using length, format and style appropriate to purpose and audience.	Writing Level 1	Generate results to a given level of accuracy using methods, measures and checking procedures appropriate to the specified purpose – use common measures.	Calculating and manipulating mathematical information Level 1
i. cash point security procedures are followed at all times	Read and obtain information from different sources.	Reading Level 1		
j. low levels of change are identified and reported in time to avoid shortages	Speak to communicate information, ideas and opinions adapting speech and content to take account of the listener(s) and medium.	Speaking and Listening Level 1	Generate results to a given level of accuracy using methods, measures and checking procedures appropriate to the specified purpose – use common measures.	Calculating and manipulating mathematical information Level 1

Unit 208: Develop and maintain effective team work and relationships

Element 208.1: Develop and maintain effective team work and relationships with colleagues

National Standard of Work	Literacy National Standard	Level Title	Numeracy National Standard	Level Title
a. requests for assistance in providing salon services are responded to willingly and courteously	Listen and respond to spoken language, including information and narratives, and follow explanations and instructions of varying length, adapting response to speaker, medium and context.	Speaking and Listening Level 1		
b. requests to others are clear and made in a courteous manner	Speak to communicate information, ideas and opinions adapting speech and content to take account of the listener(s) and medium.	Speaking and Listening Level 1		
c. the needs of others are anticipated where possible and assistance is offered promptly	Engage in discussion with one or more people in a variety of different situations, making clear and effective contributions that produce outcomes appropriate to purpose and topic.	Speaking and Listening Level 2		
d. the type of assistance given to your colleagues meets your job responsibilities	Read and obtain information of varying length and detail from different sources.	Reading Level 2		
e. the extent of assistance given to your colleagues meets the needs of your working arrangements and is within the limits of your own authority	Read and obtain information of varying length and detail from different sources.	Reading Level 2		
f. unclear information and instructions are clarified with the relevant person	Engage in discussion with one or more people in familiar and unfamiliar situations, making clear and relevant contributions that respond to what others say and produce a shared understanding about different topics.	Speaking and Listening Level 1		
g. problems likely to affect salon services are accurately reported to the relevant person	Speak to communicate information, ideas and opinions adapting speech and content to take account of the listener(s) and medium.	Speaking and Listening Level 1		

Getting the basics right in Hairdressing

National Standard of Work	Literacy National Standard	Level Title	Numeracy National Standard	Level Title
h. your own actions at work contribute to the promotion of harmony within the team	N/A			

Unit 208: Develop and maintain effective team work and relationships

Element 208.2: Develop and improve personal effectiveness within the job role

National Standard of Work	Literacy National Standard	Level Title	Numeracy National Standard	Level Title
a. your own strengths and weaknesses within the job role are identified and agreed with the relevant person	Engage in discussion with one or more people in a variety of different situations, making clear and effective contributions that produce outcomes appropriate to purpose and topic. Write to communicate information, ideas and opinions clearly and effectively, using length, format and style appropriate to purpose, content and audience.	Speaking and Listening Level 2 Writing Level 2		
b. the identification of your own strengths and weaknesses is based on salon and National Occupational Standards	Read and obtain information of varying length and detail from different sources.	Reading Level 2		
c. ways of improving your own performance are identified with the relevant person and realistic targets agreed	Engage in discussion with one or more people in familiar and unfamiliar situations, making clear and relevant contributions that respond to what others say and produce a shared understanding about different topics.	Speaking and Listening Level 1		
d. opportunities for self development are used to best effect	N/A			
e. progress towards the achievement of agreed targets is regularly reviewed	Engage in discussion with one or more people in familiar and unfamiliar situations, making clear and relevant contributions that respond to what others say and produce a shared understanding about different topics.	Speaking and Listening Level 1		
f. the results of reviews are used constructively to help personal development	N/A			

Getting the basics right in Hairdressing

National Standard of Work	Literacy National Standard	Level Title	Numeracy National Standard	Level Title
g. any problems relating to your own work role are identified and resolved with the relevant person	Engage in discussion with one or more people in a variety of different situations, making clear and effective contributions that produce outcomes appropriate to purpose and topic.	Speaking and Listening Level 2		
h. developments in hairdressing and related areas are regularly reviewed	Read and obtain information of varying length and detail from different sources.

Engage in discussion with one or more people in a variety of different situations, making clear and effective contributions that produce outcomes appropriate to purpose and topic. | Reading Level 2

Speaking and Listening Level 2 | | |

Unit 209: Support health, safety and security of the salon environment

Element 209.1: Follow emergency procedures

National Standard of Work	Literacy National Standard	Level Title	Numeracy National Standard	Level Title
a. fire and evacuation procedures are followed as specified	Read and obtain information of varying length and detail from different sources.	Reading Level 2		
b. clients and visitors are assisted to ensure prompt and safe evacuation to specified assembly points	Speak to communicate straight-forward and detailed information, ideas and opinions clearly, adapting speech and content to take account of the listener(s), medium, purpose and situation.	Speaking and Listening Level 2		
c. the named emergency personnel are accurately identified and located	Read and obtain information from different sources.	Reading Level 1		
d. fire fighting equipment is accurately identified and located				
e. specified first aid and accident reporting procedures are correctly followed	Read and obtain information of varying length and detail from different sources.	Reading Level 2		
f. accident reports concerning yourself and any of your clients are accurate and complete	Write to communicate information, ideas and opinions clearly and effectively, using length, format and style appropriate to purpose, content and audience.	Writing Level 2		
g. requests for emergency assistance are made promptly to the relevant person	Speak to communicate information, ideas and opinions adapting speech and content to take account of the listener(s) and medium.	Speaking and Listening Level 1		

Unit 209: Support health, safety and security of the salon environment

Element 209.2: Support health, safety and security at work

National Standard of Work	Literacy National Standard	Level Title	Numeracy National Standard	Level Title
a. your clothing, hair and accessories do not endanger the health and safety of yourself and others and meet salon requirements	Read and understand straightforward texts of varying length on a variety of topics accurately and independently.	Reading Level 1		
b. your personal conduct around the workplace does not endanger the health and safety of yourself and others	N/A			
c. your posture and deportment whilst working minimises the risk of harm and injury	Read and obtain information from different sources.	Reading Level 1		
d. your methods of manually lifting and handling items minimise the risk of injury				
e. the procedures for maintaining the security of the premises and contents are correctly followed	Read and obtain information from different sources.	Reading Level 1		
f. breaches of security are promptly reported to the relevant person	Speak to communicate information, ideas and opinions adapting speech and content to take account of the listener(s) and medium. Write to communicate information, ideas and opinions clearly, using length, format and style appropriate to purpose and audience.	Speaking and Listening Level 1 Writing Level 1		
g. hazards are identified and removed, if possible, within limits of your own authority	Read and obtain information of varying length and detail from different sources.	Reading Level 2		
h. hazards which cannot be removed are referred promptly to the relevant person	Speak to communicate information, ideas and opinions adapting speech and content to take account of the listener(s) and medium.	Speaking and Listening Level 1		

Unit 209: Support health, safety and security of the salon environment

Element 209.2: Support health, safety and security at work *(continued)*

National Standard of Work	Literacy National Standard	Level Title	Numeracy National Standard	Level Title
i. any potentially infectious personal condition are reported to the relevant person at the first opportunity	Speak to communicate information, ideas and opinions adapting speech and content to take account of the listener(s) and medium.	Speaking and Listening Level 1		

Unit 210: Cut hair using barbering techniques

Element 210.1: Maintain effective and safe methods of working when cutting hair using barbering techniques

National Standard of Work	Literacy National Standard	Level Title	Numeracy National Standard	Level Title
a. the preparation of the client meets salon requirements	N/A			
b. the tools used are suitable for achieving the desired look	N/A			
c. your work methods ensure the health and safety of the client and yourself	Read and obtain information of varying length and detail from different sources.	Reading Level 2		
d. the organisation of your work activities ensures effective use of all working time			Generate results to a given level of accuracy using methods, measures and checking procedures appropriate to the specified purpose – use common measures.	Calculating and manipulating mathematical information Level 1
e. the work area is kept clean, tidy and free of waste	N/A			
f. your work methods minimise the risk of damage to tools	N/A			
g. your standards of health and hygiene minimise risk of cross infection and infestation	Read and obtain information of varying length and detail from different sources.	Reading Level 2		
h. used sharps are disposed of to meet legal and salon requirements	Read and obtain information of varying length and detail from different sources.	Reading Level 2		

Unit 210: Cut hair using barbering techniques

Element 210.2: Cut hair to achieve a variety of looks with different neckline shapes

National Standard of Work	Literacy National Standard	Level Title	Numeracy National Standard	Level Title
a. preparation activities meet salon, service and legal requirements	Read and obtain information of varying length and detail from different sources.	Reading Level 2		
b. the desired look is confirmed with the client prior to cutting	Speak to communicate information, ideas and opinions adapting speech and content to take account of the listener(s) and medium.	Speaking and Listening Level 1		
c. your cutting techniques are adapted to take account of critical influencing factors, hair type and the cutting effect required	Read and understand a range of texts of varying complexity accurately and independently.	Reading Level 2		
d. the finished cut, where necessary, ensures that natural and added hair blend effectively	N/A			
e. hair cuttings which may affect the comfort of the client are promptly removed	N/A			
f. the client is consulted during the cutting process to confirm the desired look	Engage in discussion with one or more people in familiar and unfamiliar situations, making clear and relevant contributions that respond to what others say and produce a shared understanding about different topics.	Speaking and Listening Level 1		
g. the neckline shapes are accurate and take account of the natural hairline	N/A			
h. the outlines are accurate and unwanted hair outside the desired outline shape is removed	N/A			
i. the sideburns are balanced and shaped to meet the client's requirements	N/A			

National Standard of Work	Literacy National Standard	Level Title	Numeracy National Standard	Level Title
j. the finished look is cut accurately and to the satisfaction of the client	Engage in discussion with one or more people in familiar and unfamiliar situations, making clear and relevant contributions that respond to what others say and produce a shared understanding about different topics.	Speaking and Listening Level 1		

Unit 211: Provide shaving and face massage services

Element 211.1: Maintain effective and safe methods of working when shaving and massaging the face

National Standard of Work	Literacy National Standard	Level Title	Numeracy National Standard	Level Title
a. the preparation of the client meets salon requirements	N/A			
b. products, tools and equipment used are based on consultation with the client and are suitable for achieving the desired result	Engage in discussion with one or more people in a variety of different situations, making clear and effective contributions that produce outcomes appropriate to purpose and topic. Read and obtain information from different sources.	Speaking and Listening Level 2 Reading Level 1		
c. fixed blade razors, where used, are correctly and safely honed and stropped as required	N/A			
d. your work methods ensure the health and safety of the client and yourself	Read and obtain information of varying length and detail from different sources.	Reading Level 2		
e. personal protective equipment is used to meet local bye-law and salon requirements	Read and obtain information from different sources.	Reading Level 1		
f. the organisation of your work activities ensures effective use of all working time			Generate results to a given level of accuracy using methods, measures and checking procedures appropriate to the specified purpose – use common measures.	Calculating and manipulating mathematical information Level 1
g. the work area is kept clean, tidy and free of waste	N/A			
h. low levels of sundries are replenished as required			Generate results to a given level of accuracy using given methods, measures and checking procedures appropriate to the specified purpose.	Calculating and manipulating mathematical information Entry 3

National Standard of Work	Literacy National Standard	Level Title	Numeracy National Standard	Level Title
i. products which need to be re-ordered are identified and reported to the relevant person	Speak to communicate information, ideas and opinions adapting speech and content to take account of the listener(s) and medium. Write to communicate information, ideas and opinions adapting speech and content to take account of the listener(s) and medium.	Speaking and Listening Level 1 Writing Level 1		
j. your work methods minimise wastage and the risk of damage to tools and equipment	N/A			
k. sharps and waste are disposed of to meet legal and salon requirements	Read and obtain information of varying length and detail from different sources.	Reading Level 2		
l. standards of health and hygiene minimise the risk of cross infection and infestation	Read and obtain information of varying length and detail from different sources.	Reading Level 2		

Unit 211: Provide shaving and face massage services

Element 211.2: Remove hair by shaving

National Standard of Work	Literacy National Standard	Level Title	Numeracy National Standard	Level Title
a. preparation activities meet salon, service and legal requirements	Read and understand straightforward texts of varying length on a variety of topics accurately and independently.	Reading Level 1		
b. the desired finished look is confirmed with the client prior to shaving	Engage in discussion with one or more people in familiar and unfamiliar situations, making clear and relevant contributions that respond to what others say and produce a shared understanding about different topics.	Speaking and Listening Level 1		
c. the condition of fixed blade razors, where used, is maintained during the shaving service	N/A			
d. the application of lather and hot towels softens the beard and relaxes the facial muscles as required	N/A			
e. the skin is adequately lubricated for shaving	N/A			
f. your shaving techniques are adapted to take account of critical influencing factors and avoid damage to the client's and your own skin	Read and understand a range of texts of varying complexity accurately and independently.	Reading Level 2		
g. the client's position is adjusted and shaving techniques are adapted and repeated as necessary throughout the shaving process to ensure safety and the effective removal of hair	N/A			
h. the client's skin is left free from lather and excess moisture after shaving	N/A			

Getting the basics right in Hairdressing

National Standard of Work	Literacy National Standard	Level Title	Numeracy National Standard	Level Title
i. finishing products, where used, are effectively applied and achieve the desired effect	Read and understand straightforward texts of varying length on a variety of topics accurately and independently.	Reading Level 1		
j. the completed shaving service is to the satisfaction of the client	Engage in discussion with one or more people in familiar and unfamiliar situations, making clear and relevant contributions that respond to what others say and produce a shared understanding about different topics.	Speaking and Listening Level 1		
k. any problems identified during the shaving process are resolved, if possible, within limits of your own authority	Engage in discussion with one or more people in familiar and unfamiliar situations, making clear and relevant contributions that respond to what others say and produce a shared understanding about different topics.	Speaking and Listening Level 1		
l. problems which cannot be resolved are referred promptly to the relevant person for action	Speak to communicate information, ideas and opinions adapting speech and content to take account of the listener(s) and medium.	Speaking and Listening Level 1		

Unit 211: Provide shaving and face massage services

Element 211.3: Massage the face

National Standard of Work	Literacy National Standard	Level Title	Numeracy National Standard	Level Title
a. preparation activities meet salon and service requirements	Read and obtain information from different sources.	Reading Level 1		
b. the desired finished result is confirmed with the client prior to massaging the face	Engage in discussion with one or more people in familiar and unfamiliar situations, making clear and relevant contributions that respond to what others say and produce a shared understanding about different topics.	Speaking and Listening Level 1		
c. the application of hot towels opens the pores and relaxes the facial muscles as required	N/A			
d. the use of massage cream achieves adequate lubrication of the skin	N/A			
e. massage techniques used achieve the required degree of skin stimulation and avoids discomfort to the client	N/A			
f. the skin is left free from massage cream and excess moisture at the end of the massage	N/A			
g. the result achieved is to the satisfaction of the client	Engage in discussion with one or more people in familiar and unfamiliar situations, making clear and relevant contributions that respond to what others say and produce a shared understanding about different topics.	Speaking and Listening Level 1		

Getting the basics right in Hairdressing

Unit 212: Cut facial hair to shape

Element 212.1: Maintain effective and safe methods of working when cutting facial hair

National Standard of Work	Literacy National Standard	Level Title	Numeracy National Standard	Level Title
a. the preparation of the client meets salon requirements	N/A			
b. tools used are based on consultation with the client and suitable for achieving the desired shape	Engage in discussion with one or more people in familiar and unfamiliar situations, making clear and relevant contributions that respond to what others say and produce a shared understanding about different topics.	Speaking and Listening Level 1		
c. your work methods ensure the health and safety of the client and yourself	Read and obtain information of varying length and detail from different sources.	Reading Level 2		
d. the organisation of your work activities ensures effective use of all working time			Generate results to a given level of accuracy using methods, measures and checking procedures appropriate to the specified purpose – use common measures.	Calculating and manipulating mathematical information Level 1
e. the work area is kept clean, tidy and free of waste	N/A			
f. your work methods minimise the risk of damage to tools	N/A			
g. your standards of health and hygiene minimise risk of cross infection and infestation	Read and obtain information of varying length and detail from different sources.	Reading Level 2		
h. used sharps are disposed of to meet legislative and salon requirements	Read and obtain information of varying length and detail from different sources.	Reading Level 2		

Unit 212: Cut facial hair to shape

Element 212.2: Cut beards and moustaches to shape

National Standard of Work	Literacy National Standard	Level Title	Numeracy National Standard	Level Title
a. preparation activities meet salon, service and legal requirements	Read and obtain information of varying length and detail from different sources.	Reading Level 2		
b. the desired finished look is confirmed with the client prior to cutting	Engage in discussion with one or more people in familiar and unfamiliar situations, making clear and relevant contributions that respond to what others say and produce a shared understanding about different topics.	Speaking and Listening Level 1		
c. the cutting techniques used are suitable for achieving the desired shape	N/A			
d. your cutting techniques are adapted to take into account critical influencing factors	Read and obtain information of varying length and detail from different sources.	Reading Level 2		
e. outlines, where required, are accurate and hair outside the desired shape is removed	N/A			
f. hair cuttings affecting the comfort of the client are promptly removed	N/A			
g. the finished shape of the facial hair is to the satisfaction of the client	Engage in discussion with one or more people in familiar and unfamiliar situations, making clear and relevant contributions that respond to what others say and produce a shared understanding about different topics.	Speaking and Listening Level 1		

Unit 213: Dry hair into shape and create a finished look

Element 213.1:   Maintain effective and safe methods of working when drying hair

National Standard of Work	Literacy National Standard	Level Title	Numeracy National Standard	Level Title
a. the preparation of the client meets salon requirements	N/A			
b. the products, tools and equipment used are based on consultation with the client and are suitable for achieving the desired look	Engage in discussion with one or more people in familiar and unfamiliar situations, making clear and relevant contributions that respond to what others say and produce a shared understanding about different topics.	Speaking and Listening Level 1		
c. your work methods ensure the health and safety of the client and yourself	Read and obtain information of varying length and detail from different sources.	Reading Level 2		
d. the organisation of your work activities ensures effective use of all working time			Generate results to a given level of accuracy using methods, measures and checking procedures appropriate to the specified purpose – use common measures.	Calculating and manipulating mathematical information Level 1
e. the work area is kept clean, tidy and free of waste	N/A			
g. your standards of health and hygiene minimise the risk of cross infection and infestation	Read and obtain information of varying length and detail from different sources.	Reading Level 2		
h. low levels of products are identified and reported to the relevant person	Speak to communicate information, ideas and opinions adapting speech and content to take account of the listener(s) and medium. Write to communicate information, ideas and opinions clearly using length, format and style appropriate to purpose and audience.	Speaking and Listening Level 1 Writing Level 1	Generate results to a given level of accuracy using methods, measures and checking procedures appropriate to the specified purpose – use common measures.	Calculating and manipulating mathematical information Entry 3

Unit 213: Dry hair into shape and create a finished look

Element 213.2: Dry and finish hair

National Standard of Work	Literacy National Standard	Level Title	Numeracy National Standard	Level Title
a. preparation activities meet salon, service and legal requirements	Read and obtain information of varying length and detail from different sources.	Reading Level 2		
b. the desired finished look is confirmed with the client before drying	Engage in discussion with one or more people in familiar and unfamiliar situations, making clear and relevant contributions that respond to what others say and produce a shared understanding about different topics.	Speaking and Listening Level 1		
c. the drying and finishing techniques used are suitable for achieving the desired look	Read and obtain information from different sources.	Reading Level 1		
d. the drying and finishing techniques are adapted to take account of critical influencing factors	Read and obtain information of varying length and detail from different sources.	Reading Level 2		
e. the application of products, when used, meets manufacturers' instructions	Read and obtain information of varying length and detail from different sources.	Reading Level 2		
f. the client is consulted during the drying and finishing process to confirm the desired look	Speak to communicate information, ideas and opinions adapting speech and content to take account of the listener(s) and medium	Speaking and Listening Level 1		
g. the client's position is adjusted and drying techniques are adapted as necessary to assist styling	N/A			
h. the finished look is to the satisfaction of the client	Engage in discussion with one or more people in familiar and unfamiliar situations, making clear and relevant contributions that respond to what others say and produce a shared understanding about different topics.	Speaking and Listening Level 1		

Getting the basics right in Hairdressing

7. Progression from the Adult Literacy Standards to the Adult Literacy Core Curriculum

National Standards for Adult Literacy

The progression between capabilities

Entry Level		

ENTRY LEVEL 1	ENTRY LEVEL 2	ENTRY LEVEL 3
Speaking and listening *At this level, adults can*	***Speaking and listening*** *At this level, adults can*	***Speaking and listening*** *At this level, adults can*
listen and respond to spoken language, including simple narratives, statements, questions and single-step instructions	**listen and respond** to spoken language, including straightforward information, short narratives, explanations and instructions	**listen and respond** to spoken language, including straightforward information and narratives, and follow straightforward explanations and instructions, both face to face and on the telephone
speak to communicate basic information, feelings and opinions on familiar topics	**speak to communicate** information, feelings and opinions on familiar topics	**speak to communicate** information, feelings and opinions on familiar topics, using appropriate formality, both face to face and on the telephone
engage in discussion with another person in a familiar situation about familiar topics	**engage in discussion** with one or more people in a familiar situation to establish shared understanding about familiar topics	**engage in discussion** with one or more people in a familiar situation, making relevant points and responding to what others say to reach a shared understanding about familiar topics
Reading *At this level, adults can*	***Reading*** *At this level, adults can*	***Reading*** *At this level, adults can*
read and understand short texts with repeated language patterns on familiar topics	**read and understand** short, straightforward texts on familiar topics	**read and understand** short, straightforward texts on familiar topics accurately and independently
read and obtain information from common signs and symbols	**read and obtain information** from short documents, familiar sources and signs and symbols	**read and obtain information** from everyday sources
Writing *At this level, adults can*	***Writing*** *At this level, adults can*	***Writing*** *At this level, adults can*
write to communicate information to an intended audience	**write to communicate** information with some awareness of the intended audience	**write to communicate** information and opinions with some adaptation to the intended audience

Getting the basics right in Hairdressing

Level 1	Level 2
Speaking and listening *At this level, adults can*	***Speaking and listening*** *At this level, adults can*
listen and respond to spoken language, including information and narratives, and follow explanations and instructions of varying lengths, adapting response to speaker, medium and context	**listen and respond** to spoken language, including extended information and narratives, and follow detailed explanations and multi-step instructions of varying length, adapting response to speaker, medium and context
speak to communicate information, ideas and opinions adapting speech and content to take account of the listener(s) and medium	**speak to communicate** straightforward and detailed information, ideas and opinions clearly, adapting speech and content to take account of the listener(s), medium, purpose and situation
engage in discussion with one or more people in familiar and unfamiliar situations, making clear and relevant contributions that respond to what others say and produce a shared understanding about different topics	**engage in discussion** with one or more people in a variety of different situations, making clear and effective contributions that produce outcomes appropriate to purpose and topic
Reading *At this level, adults can*	***Reading*** *At this level, adults can*
read and understand straightforward texts of varying length on a variety of topics accurately and independently	**read and understand** a range of texts of varying complexity accurately and independently
read and obtain information from different sources	**read and obtain information** of varying length and detail from different sources
Writing *At this level, adults can*	***Writing*** *At this level, adults can*
write to communicate information, ideas and opinions clearly using length, format and style appropriate to purpose and audience	**write to communicate** information, ideas and opinions clearly and effectively, using length, format and style appropriate to purpose, content and audience

Speaking and listening: the progression between curriculum elements

Entry Level		
TEXT FOCUS	**ENTRY 1 LEVEL**	**ENTRY 2 LEVEL**
Listen and respond	**SLlr/E1.1** Listen for the gist of short explanations **SLlr/E1.2** Listen for detail using key words to extract some specific information **SLlr/E1.3** Follow single-step instructions in a familiar context, asking for instructions to be repeated if necessary **SLlr/E1.4** Listen and respond to requests for personal information	**SLlr/E2.1** Listen for and follow the gist of explanations, instructions and narratives **SLlr/E2.2** Listen for detail in short explanations, instructions and narratives **SLlr/E2.3** Listen for and identify the main points of short explanations or presentations **SLlr/E2.4** Listen to and follow short, straightforward explanations and instructions **SLlr/E2.5** Listen to and identify simply expressed feelings and opinions **SLlr/E2.6** Respond to straightforward questions
Speak to communicate	**SLc/E1.1** Speak clearly to be heard and understood in simple exchanges **SLc/E1.2** Make requests using appropriate terms **SLc/E1.3** Ask questions to obtain specific information **SLc/E1.4** Make statements of fact clearly	**SLc/E2.1** Speak clearly to be heard and understood in straightforward exchanges **SLc/E2.2** Make requests and ask questions to obtain information in everyday contexts **SLc/E2.3** Express clearly statements of fact, and short accounts and descriptions **SLc/E2.4** Ask questions to clarify understanding
Engage in discussion	**SLd/E1.1** Speak and listen in simple exchanges and everyday contexts	**SLd/E2.1** Follow the gist of discussions **SLd/E2.2** Follow the main points and make appropriate contributions to the discussion

(Entry Level 3)	(Level 1)	(Level 2)
SLlr/E3.1 Listen for and follow the gist of explanations, instructions and narratives in different contexts **SLlr/E3.2** Listen for detail in explanations, instructions and narratives in different contexts **SLlr/E3.3** Listen for and identify relevant information and new information from discussions, explanations and presentations **SLlr/E3.4** Use strategies to clarify and confirm understanding (e.g. facial expressions or gestures) **SLlr/E3.5** Listen to and respond appropriately to other points of view **SLlr/E3.6** Respond to a range of questions about familiar topics	**SLlr/L1.1** Listen for and identify relevant information from explanations and presentations on a range of straightforward topics **SLlr/L1.2** Listen for and understand explanations, instructions and narratives on different topics in a range of contexts **SLlr/L1.3** Use strategies to clarify and confirm understanding (e.g. facial expressions, body language and verbal prompts) **SLlr/L1.4** Provide feedback and confirmation when listening to others **SLlr/L1.5** Make contributions relevant to the situation and the subject **SLlr/L1.6** Respond to questions on a range of topics	**SLlr/L2.1** Listen for and identify relevant information from extended explanations or presentations on a range of topics **SLlr/L2.2** Listen to, understand and follow lengthy or multi-step instructions and narratives on a range of topics and in a range of contexts **SLlr/L2.3** Respond to detailed or extended questions on a range of topics **SLlr/L2.4** Respond to criticism and criticise constructively
SLc/E3.1 Speak clearly to be heard and understood using appropriate clarity, speed and phrasing **SLc/E3.2** Use formal language and register when appropriate **SLc/E3.3** Express clearly statements of fact and give short explanations, accounts and descriptions **SLc/E3.4** Make requests and ask questions to obtain information in familiar and unfamiliar contexts	**SLc/L1.1** Speak clearly in a way which suits the situation **SLc/L1.2** Make requests and ask questions to obtain information in familiar and unfamiliar contexts **SLc/L1.3** Express clearly statements of fact, explanations, instructions, accounts, and descriptions **SLc/L1.4** Present information and ideas in a logical sequence and include detail and develop ideas where appropriate	**SLc/L2.1** Speak clearly and confidently in a way which suits the situation **SLc/L2.2** Make requests and ask questions to obtain detailed information in familiar and unfamiliar contexts **SLc/L2.3** Express clearly statements of fact, explanations, instructions, accounts, descriptions using appropriate structure, style and vocabulary **SLc/L2.4** Present information and ideas in a logical sequence and provide further detail and development to clarify or confirm understanding
SLd/E3.1 Follow and understand the main points of discussions on different topics **SLd/E3.2** Make contributions to discussions that are relevant to the subject **SLd/E3.3** Respect the turn-taking rights of others during discussions	**SLd/L1.1** Follow and contribute to discussions on a range of straightforward topics **SLd/L1.2** Respect the turn-taking rights of others during discussions **SLd/L1.3** Use appropriate phrases for interruption	**SLd/L2.1** Make relevant contributions and help to move discussions forward **SLd/L2.2** Adapt contributions to discussions to suit audience, context, purpose and situation **SLd/L2.3** Use appropriate phrases for interruption and change of topic **SLd/L2.4** Support opinions and arguments with evidence **SLd/L2.5** Use strategies intended to reassure (e.g. body language and appropriate phraseology)

Reading and Writing (Text focus): the progression between curriculum elements

READING ☐   WRITING ▨

	Entry Level	

TEXT FOCUS	ENTRY 1 LEVEL	ENTRY 2 LEVEL
Reading comprehension	**Rt/E1.1** Follow a short narrative on a familiar topic or experience **Rt/E1.2** Recognise the different purposes of texts at this level	**Rt/E2.1** Trace and understand the main events of chronological and instructional texts **Rt/E2.2** Recognise the different purposes of texts at this level **Rt/E2.3** Identify common sources of information **Rt/E2.4** Use illustrations and captions to locate information
Writing composition	**Wt/E1.1** Use written words and phrases to record or present information	**Wt/E2.1** Use written words and phrases to record or present information

ENTRY LEVEL 3	LEVEL 1	LEVEL 2
Rt/E3.1 Trace and understand the main events of chronological, continuous descriptive and explanatory texts of more than one paragraph	**Rt/L1.1** Trace and understand the main events of continuous descriptive, explanatory and persuasive texts	**Rt/L2.1** Trace and understand the main events of continuous descriptive, explanatory and persuasive texts
Rt/E3.2 Recognise the different purposes of texts at this level	**Rt/L1.2** Recognise how language and other textual features are used to achieve different purposes (e.g. to instruct, explain, describe, persuade)	**Rt/L2.2** Identify the purpose of a text and infer meaning which is not explicit
Rt/E3.3 Recognise and understand the organisational features and typical language of instructional texts (e.g. use of imperatives and second person)	**Rt/L1.3** Identify the main points and specific detail, and infer meaning from images which is not explicit in the text	**Rt/L2.3** Identify the main points and specific detail
Rt/E3.4 Identify the main points and ideas, and predict words from context	**Rt/L1.4** Use organisational and structural features to locate information (e.g. contents, index, menus, subheadings, paragraphs)	**Rt/L2.4** Read an argument and identify the points of view
Rt/E3.5 Understand and use organisational features to locate information (e.g. contents, index, menus)	**Rt/L1.5** Use different reading strategies to find and obtain information	**Rt/L2.5** Read critically to evaluate information, and compare information, ideas and opinions from different sources
Rt/E3.6 Skim read title, headings and illustrations to decide if material is of interest		**Rt/L2.6** Use organisational features and systems to locate texts and information
Rt/E3.7 Scan texts to locate information		**Rt/L2.7** Use different reading strategies to find and obtain information (e.g. skimming, scanning, detailed reading)
Rt/E3.8 Obtain specific information through detailed reading		**Rt/L2.8** Summarise information from longer documents
Rt/E3.9 Relate an image to print and use it to obtain meaning		
Wt/E3.1 Plan and draft writing	**Wt/L1.1** Plan and draft writing	**Wt/L2.1** Plan and draft writing
Wt/E3.2 Organise writing in short paragraphs	**Wt/L1.2** Judge how much to write and the level of detail to include	**Wt/L2.2** Judge how much to write and the level of detail to include
Wt/E3.3 Sequence chronological writing	**Wt/L1.3** Present information in a logical sequence using paragraphs where appropriate	**Wt/L2.3** Present information and ideas in a logical or persuasive sequence, using paragraphs where appropriate
Wt/E3.4 Proof read and correct writing for grammar and spelling	**Wt/L1.4** Use language suitable for purpose and audience	**Wt/L2.4** Use format and structure to organise writing for different purposes
	Wt/L1.5 Use format and structure for different purposes	**Wt/L2.5** Use formal and informal language appropriate to purpose and audience
	Wt/L1.6 Proof-read and revise writing for accuracy and meaning	**Wt/L2.6** Use different styles of writing for different purposes (e.g. persuasive techniques, supporting evidence, technical vocabulary)
		Wt/L2.7 Proof-read and revise writing for accuracy and meaning

Reading and Writing (Sentence focus): the progression between curriculum elements

READING ☐   WRITING ▩

Entry Level		
TEXT FOCUS	**ENTRY 1 LEVEL**	**ENTRY 2 LEVEL**
Grammar and punctuation	**Rs/E1.1** Read and recognise simple sentence structures	**Rs/E2.1** Read and understand linking words and adverbials in instructions and directions (e.g. *next, then, right* and *straight on*) **Rs/E2.2** Use knowledge of simple sentence structure and word order to help decipher unfamiliar words and predict meaning **Rs/E2.3** Apply own life experience and knowledge to check out plausible meanings of a sentence as a whole when decoding unfamiliar words **Rs/E2.4** Use punctuation and capitalisation to aid understanding
Grammar and punctuation	**Ws/E1.1** Construct a simple sentence **Ws/E1.2** Punctuate a simple sentence with a capital letter and a full stop **Ws/E1.3** Use a capital letter for personal pronoun 'I'	**Ws/E2.1** Construct simple and compound sentences, using common conjunctions to connect two clauses (e.g. *as, and, but*) **Ws/E2.2** Use adjectives **Ws/E2.3** Use punctuation correctly (e.g. capital letters, full stops and question marks) **Ws/E2.4** Use a capital letter for proper nouns

ENTRY LEVEL 3	LEVEL 1	 LEVEL 2
Rs/E3.1 Recognise and understand the organisational features and typical language of instructional texts (e.g. use of imperatives, second person) **Rs/E3.2** Use implicit and explicit knowledge of different types of word (e.g. linking words [connectives], nouns, verbs, adjectives), of word order, and of possible plausible meanings, to help decode unfamiliar words and predict meaning **Rs/E3.3** Use punctuation and capitalisation to aid understanding	**Rs/L1.1** Use implicit and explicit grammatical knowledge (e.g. of different sentence forms, types of word, verb tense, word order) along with own knowledge and experience to predict meaning, try out plausible meanings, and to read and check for sense **Rs/L1.2** Use punctuation to help their understanding	**Rs/L2.1** Use implicit and explicit grammatical knowledge, alongside own knowledge and experience of context, to help follow meaning and judge the purpose of different types of text **Rs/L2.2** Use punctuation to help interpret the meaning and purpose of texts
Ws/E3.1 Write in complete sentences **Ws/E3.2** Use correct basic grammar (e.g. appropriate verb tense, subject–verb agreement) **Ws/E3.3** Use punctuation correctly (e.g. capital letters, full stops, question marks, exclamation marks)	**Ws/L1.1** Write in complete sentences **Ws/L1.2** Use correct grammar (e.g. subject–verb agreement, correct use of tense) **Ws/L1.3** Punctuate sentences correctly, and use punctuation so that meaning is clear	**Ws/L2.1** Construct complex sentences **Ws/L2.2** Use correct grammar (e.g. subject – verb agreement, correct and consistent use of tense) **Ws/L2.3** Use pronouns so that their meaning is clear **Ws/L2.4** Punctuate sentences correctly, and use punctuation accurately (e.g. commas, apostrophes, inverted commas)

Reading and Writing (Word focus): the progression between curriculum elements

READING ☐   WRITING ▨

Entry Level		
TEXT FOCUS	**ENTRY 1 LEVEL**	**ENTRY 2 LEVEL**
Vocabulary, word recognition and phonics	**Rw/E1.1** Possess a limited, meaningful sight vocabulary of words, signs and symbols **Rw/E1.2** Decode simple, regular words **Rw/E1.3** Recognise the letters of the alphabet in both upper and lower case	**Rw/E2.1** Read and understand words on forms related to personal information (e.g. first name, surname, address, postcode, age, date of birth) **Rw/E2.2** Recognise high-frequency words and words with common spelling patterns **Rw/E2.3** Use phonic and graphic knowledge to decode words **Rw/E2.4** Use a simplified dictionary to find the meaning of unfamiliar words **Rw/E2.5** Use initial letters to find and sequence words in alphabetical order
Spelling and handwriting	**Ww/E1.1** Spell correctly some personal key words and familiar words **Ww/E1.2** Write the letters of the alphabet using upper and lower case **Ww/E1.3** Use basic sound–symbol association to help spelling, *as appropriate for the needs of the learner*	**Ww/E2.1** Spell correctly the majority of personal details and familiar common words **Ww/E2.2** Use their knowledge of sound–symbol relationships and phonological patterns (e.g. consonant clusters and vowel phonemes) to help work out correct spellings, *as appropriate for the needs of the learner* **Ww/E2.3** Produce legible text

![Entry 3 Level]	![Level 1]	![Level 2]
Rw/E3.1 Recognise and understand relevant specialist key words **Rw/E3.2** Read and understand words and phrases commonly used on forms **Rw/E3.3** Use a dictionary to find the meaning of unfamiliar words **Rw/E3.4** Use first- and second-place letters to find and sequence words in alphabetical order **Rw/E3.5** Use a variety of reading strategies to help decode an increasing range of unfamiliar words	**Rw/L1.1** Use reference material to find the meaning of unfamiliar words **Rw/L1.2** Recognise and understand the vocabulary associated with different types of text, using appropriate strategies to work out meaning **Rw/L1.3** Recognise and understand an increasing range of vocabulary, applying knowledge of word structure, related words, word roots, derivations, borrowings	**Rw/L2.1** Read and understand technical vocabulary **Rw/L2.2** Use reference material to find the meaning of unfamiliar words **Rw/L2.3** Recognise and understand vocabulary associated with texts of different levels of accessibility, formality, complexity and of different purpose
Ww/E3.1 Spell correctly common words and relevant key words for work and special interest **Ww/E3.2** Use their developing knowledge of sound–symbol relationships and phonological patterns to help spell a greater range of words and longer words, *as appropriate for the needs of the learner* **Ww/E3.3** Produce legible text	**Ww/L1.1** Spell correctly words used most often in work, studies and daily life **Ww/L1.2** Produce legible text	**Ww/L2.1** Spell correctly words used most often in work, studies and daily life, including familiar technical words **Ww/L2.2** Produce legible text

8. Progression from the Adult Numeracy Standards to the Adult Numeracy Core Curriculum

National Standards for Adult Numeracy

The progression between capabilities

Entry Level		
ENTRY LEVEL 1	**ENTRY LEVEL 2**	**ENTRY LEVEL 3**
Understanding and using mathematical information *At this level, adults can*	*Understanding and using mathematical information* *At this level, adults can*	*Understanding and using mathematical information* *At this level, adults can*
read and understand information given by numbers and symbols in simple graphical, numerical and written material	**read and understand** information given by numbers, symbols, simple diagrams and charts in graphical, numerical and written material	**read and understand** information given by numbers, symbols, diagrams and charts used for different purposes and in different ways in graphical, numerical and written material
specify and describe a practical problem or task using numbers and measures	**specify and describe** a practical problem or task using numbers, measures and simple shapes to record essential information	**specify and describe** a practical problem or task using numbers, measures and diagrams to collect and record relevant information
Calculating and manipulating mathematical information *At this level, adults can*	**Calculating and manipulating mathematical information** *At this level, adults can*	**Calculating and manipulating mathematical information** *At this level, adults can*
generate results which make sense and use given methods and given checking procedures appropriate to the specified purpose	**generate results** to a given level of accuracy using given methods and given checking procedures appropriate to the specified purpose	**generate results** to a given level of accuracy using given methods, measures and checking procedures appropriate to the specified purpose
Interpreting results and communicating mathematical information *At this level, adults can*	*Interpreting results and communicating mathematical information* *At this level, adults can*	*Interpreting results and communicating mathematical information* *At this level, adults can*
present and explain results which show an understanding of the intended purpose using appropriate numbers, measures, objects or pictures	**present and explain results** which meet the intended purpose using appropriate numbers, simple diagrams and symbols	**present and explain results** which meet the intended purpose using appropriate numbers, diagrams, charts and symbols

Understanding and using mathematical information *At this level, adults can*	***Understanding and using mathematical information*** *At this level, adults can*
read and understand straightforward mathematical information used for different purposes and independently select relevant information from given graphical, numerical and written material	**read and understand** mathematical information used for different purposes and independently select and compare relevant information from a variety of graphical, numerical and written material
specify and describe a practical activity, problem or task using mathematical information and language to make accurate observations and identify suitable calculations to achieve an appropriate outcome	**specify and describe** a practical activity, problem or task using mathematical information and language to increase understanding and select appropriate methods for carrying through a substantial activity
Calculating and manipulating mathematical information *At this level, adults can*	**Calculating and manipulating mathematical information** *At this level, adults can*
generate results to a given level of accuracy using methods, measures and checking procedures appropriate to the specified purpose	**generate results** to an appropriate level of accuracy using methods, measures and checking procedures appropriate to the specified purpose
Interpreting results and communicating mathematical information *At this level, adults can*	***Interpreting results and communicating mathematical information*** *At this level, adults can*
present and explain results which meet the intended purpose using an appropriate format to a given level of accuracy	**present and explain results** clearly and accurately using numerical, graphical and written formats appropriate to purpose, findings and audience

Number: the progression between curriculum elements

	Entry Level	
	ENTRY 1 LEVEL	**ENTRY 2 LEVEL**
Whole numbers	**N1/E1.1** Count reliably up to 10 items **N1/E1.2** Read and write numbers up to 10, including zero **N1/E1.3** Order and compare numbers up to 10, including zero **N1/E1.4** Add single-digit numbers with totals to 10 **N1/E1.5** Subtract single-digit numbers from numbers up to 10 **N1/E1.6** Interpret $+$, $-$ and $=$ in practical situations for solving problems **N1/E1.7** Use a calculator to check calculations using whole numbers	**N1/E2.1** Count reliably up to 20 items **N1/E2.2** Read, write, order and compare numbers up to 100 **N1/E2.3** Add and subtract two-digit whole numbers **N1/E2.4** Recall addition and subtraction facts to 10 **N1/E2.5** Multiply using single-digit whole numbers **N1/E2.6** Approximate by rounding to the nearest 10 **N1/E2.7** Use and interpret $+$, $-$, $\times$ and $\div$ in practical situations for solving problems **N1/E2.8** Use a calculator to check calculations using whole numbers
Fractions, decimals and percentages		**N2/E2.1** Read, write and compare halves and quarters of quantities **N2/E2.2** Find halves and quarters of small numbers of items or shapes

 ENTRY LEVEL 3	LEVEL 1	LEVEL 2
N1/E3.1 Count, read, write, order and compare numbers up to 1000 **N1/E3.2** Add and subtract using three-digit whole numbers **N1/E3.3** Recall addition and subtraction facts to 20 **N1/E3.4** Multiply two-digit whole numbers by single-digit whole numbers **N1/E3.5** Recall multiplication facts (e.g. multiples of 2, 3, 4, 5, 10) **N1/E3.6** Divide two-digit whole numbers by single-digit whole numbers and interpret remainders **N1/E3.7** Approximate by rounding numbers less than 1000 to the nearest 10 or 100 **N1/E3.8** Estimate answers to calculations **N1/E3.9** Use and interpret $+$, $-$, $\times$, $\div$ and $=$ in practical situations for solving problems	**N1/L1.1** Read, write, order and compare numbers, including large numbers **N1/L1.2** Recognise negative numbers in practical contexts (e.g. temperatures) **N1/L1.3** Add, subtract, multiply and divide using efficient written methods **N1/L1.4** Multiply and divide whole numbers by 10 and 100 **N1/L1.5** Recall multiplication facts up to 10×10 and make connections with division facts **N1/L1.6** Recognise numerical relationships (e.g. multiples and squares) **N1/L1.7** Work out simple ratio and direct proportion **N1/L1.8** Approximate by rounding **N1/L1.9** Estimate answers to calculations	**N1/L2.1** Read, write, order and compare positive and negative numbers of any size in a practical context **N1/L2.2** Carry out calculations with numbers of any size using efficient methods **N1/L2.3** Calculate ratio and direct proportion **N1/L2.4** Evaluate expressions and make substitutions in given formulae in words and symbols to produce results
N2/E3.1 Read, write and understand common fractions (e.g. $\frac{3}{4}$, $\frac{2}{3}$, $\frac{1}{10}$) **N2/E3.2** Recognise and use equivalent forms (e.g. $\frac{5}{10} = \frac{1}{2}$) **N2/E3.3** Read, write and understand decimals up to two decimal places in practical contexts (such as: common measures to one decimal place, e.g. 1.5 m; money in decimal notation, e.g. £2.37) **N2/E3.4** Use a calculator to calculate using whole numbers and decimals to solve problems in context, and to check calculations	**N2/L1.1** Read, write, order and compare common fractions and mixed numbers **N2/L1.2** Find parts of whole number quantities or measurements (e.g. $\frac{2}{3}$ or $\frac{3}{4}$) **N2/L1.3** Recognise equivalencies between common fractions, percentages and decimals (e.g. $50\% = \frac{1}{2}$, $0.25 = \frac{1}{4}$) and use these to find part of whole number quantities **N2/L1.4** Read, write, order and compare decimals up to three decimal places **N2/L1.5** Add, subtract, multiply and divide decimals up to two places **N2/L1.6** Multiply and divide decimals by 10, 100 **N2/L1.7** Approximate decimals by rounding to a whole number or two decimal places **N2/L1.8** Read, write, order and compare simple percentages, and understand simple percentage increase and decrease **N2/L1.9** Find simple percentage parts of quantities and measurements **N2/L1.10** Find simple percentage increase and decrease **N2/L1.11** Use a calculator to calculate efficiently using whole numbers, fractions, decimals and percentages	**N2/L2.1** Use fractions to order and compare amounts or quantities **N2/L2.2** Identify equivalencies between fractions, decimals and percentages **N2/L2.3** Evaluate one number as a fraction of another **N2/L2.4** Use fractions to add and subtract amounts or quantities **N2/L2.5** Order, approximate and compare decimals when solving practical problems **N2/L2.6** Add, subtract, multiply and divide decimals up to three places **N2/L2.7** Order and compare percentages and understand percentage increase and decrease **N2/L2.8** Find percentage parts of quantities and measurements **N2/L2.9** Evaluate one number as a percentage of another **N2/L2.10** Use a calculator to calculate efficiently using whole numbers, fractions, decimals and percentages

Measures, shape and space: the progression between curriculum elements

	Entry Level	
	ENTRY 1 LEVEL	**ENTRY 2 LEVEL**
Common measures	**MSS1/E1.1** Recognise and select coins and notes **MSS1/E1.2** Relate familiar events to: times of the day; days of the week; seasons of the year **MSS1/E1.3** Describe size and use direct comparisons for the size of at least two items **MSS1/E1.4** Describe length, width, height, and use direct comparisons for length, width and height of items **MSS1/E1.5** Describe weight and use direct comparisons for the weight of items **MSS1/E1.6** Describe capacity and use direct comparisons for the capacity of items	**MSS1/E2.1** Make amounts of money up to £1 in different ways using 1p, 2p, 5p, 10p, 20p and 50p coins **MSS1/E2.2** Calculate the cost of more than one item and the change from a transaction, in pence or in whole pounds **MSS1/E2.3** Read and record time in common date formats **MSS1/E2.4** Read and understand time displayed on analogue and 12-hour digital clocks in hours, half hours and quarter hours **MSS1/E2.5** Read, estimate, measure and compare length using common standard and non-standard units (e.g. metre, centimetre, paces) **MSS1/E2.6** Read, estimate, measure and compare weight using common standard units (e.g. kilogram) **MSS1/E2.7** Read, estimate, measure and compare capacity using common standard and non-standard units (e.g. litre, cupful) **MSS1/E2.8** Read and compare positive temperatures in everyday situations such as weather charts **MSS1/E2.9** Read simple scales to the nearest labelled division
Shape and space	**MSS2/E1.1** Recognise and name common 2-D and 3-D shapes **MSS2/E1.2** Understand everyday positional vocabulary (e.g. between, inside or near to)	**MSS2/E2.1** Recognise and name 2-D and 3-D shapes **MSS2/E2.2** Describe the properties of common 2-D and 3-D shapes **MSS2/E2.3** Use positional vocabulary